Preface

Navigating the Realm of Email Marketing

Welcome to a comprehensive exploration of the intricate world of email marketing. As businesses and individuals continue to thrive in the digital age, email marketing stands as a steadfast and powerful tool for connecting, engaging, and fostering meaningful relationships with audiences. This guide is designed to be your compass, guiding you through the diverse landscape of email marketing—from its foundational principles to advanced techniques that can propel your campaigns to new heights.

Whether you're a novice seeking to launch your very first email campaign or a seasoned marketer looking to refine your strategies, this guide has been crafted to provide actionable insights, practical advice, and real-world examples that empower you to achieve your email marketing goals. As technology evolves and consumer behaviors shift, the role of email marketing continually adapts. By embracing the wisdom contained within these pages, you can navigate these changes with confidence, mastering the art of email marketing and leveraging it as a dynamic force for growth.

Throughout this guide, you'll embark on a journey that encompasses:

Laying the foundations of a robust email marketing strategy

Crafting compelling content that resonates with your audience

Embracing the power of automation and personalization

Learning from both the successes and challenges of real-world case studies

Exploring advanced techniques like AI, interactive elements, and behavioral targeting

Email marketing is not just a collection of tactics—it's a multifaceted approach that combines creativity, strategy, and a deep understanding of your audience. As you delve into each chapter, remember that every concept, every technique, and every piece of advice is a stepping stone on your path to mastery.

So, whether you're just beginning your journey or seeking to enhance your existing expertise, prepare to be inspired, informed, and equipped with the tools you need to flourish in the realm of email marketing. As you absorb the knowledge within these pages, may you find the guidance you seek, the strategies you need, and the motivation to embark on a transformative email marketing journey that leaves a lasting impact on your business and your audience.

Table of Contents

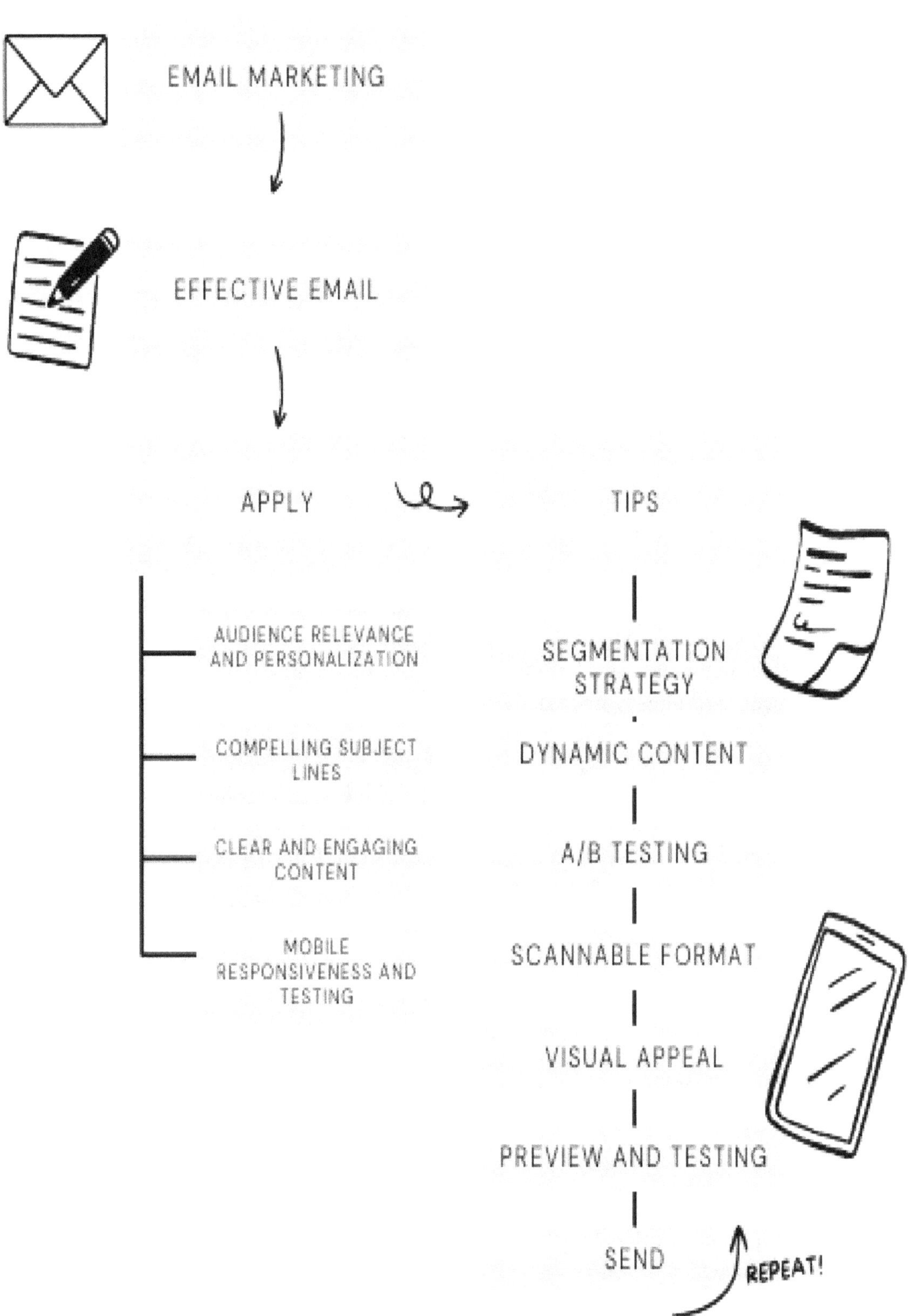

EMAIL MARKETING
EFFECTIVE EMAIL
APPLY
TIPS
AUDIENCE RELEVANCE AND PERSONALIZATION
SEGMENTATION STRATEGY
COMPELLING SUBJECT LINES
DYNAMIC CONTENT
CLEAR AND ENGAGING CONTENT
A/B TESTING
MOBILE RESPONSIVENESS AND TESTING
SCANNABLE FORMAT
VISUAL APPEAL
PREVIEW AND TESTING
SEND
REPEAT!

Introduction to Email Marketing

In the ever-evolving landscape of digital marketing, one strategy has stood the test of time and continues to deliver remarkable results: email marketing. In a world flooded with social media, paid advertisements, and content marketing, email marketing remains a steadfast and powerful tool for businesses of all sizes. With its direct and personalized approach, email marketing enables brands to establish meaningful connections with their audience, nurture leads, and drive conversions.

Definition and Importance of Email Marketing

At its core, email marketing involves sending targeted messages to a group of individuals through email. These messages can range from promotional offers and product updates to informative newsletters and personalized recommendations. The pivotal aspect that sets email marketing apart is its permission-based nature. Unlike many other marketing strategies, email marketing requires recipients to have willingly subscribed to receive communications from the sender. This opt-in process ensures that the emails are reaching an audience that is already interested and engaged with the brand, increasing the likelihood of positive responses.

The significance of email marketing cannot be overstated. While social media platforms come and go, and search engine algorithms change overnight, email remains a constant in the lives of consumers. Most individuals check their emails daily, making it an integral part of their routine. This consistent presence allows brands to establish a sense of familiarity and trust with their audience over time.

Benefits of Email Marketing for Businesses

The benefits of email marketing are multifaceted and extend far beyond mere communication. Here are a few key advantages that make email marketing an indispensable tool for businesses:

Direct Communication: Email provides a direct line of communication between brands and their customers. Messages land directly in recipients' inboxes, offering an intimate channel for delivering important information.

Personalization: Email marketing allows for high levels of personalization. By segmenting your email list and tailoring content to specific demographics or behaviors, you can deliver content that resonates with each recipient on an individual level.

Cost-Effectiveness: When compared to traditional forms of advertising, email marketing boasts an impressive return on investment (ROI). The costs associated with sending emails are relatively low, making it a cost-effective marketing strategy.

Trackable Metrics: Email marketing platforms offer robust analytics that enable marketers to track open rates, click-through rates, conversion rates, and more. This data empowers businesses to refine their strategies and optimize their campaigns for better results.

Engagement and Conversion: Emails have the potential to drive high levels of engagement and conversions. Well-crafted emails with compelling content and clear calls-to-action can lead recipients down the sales funnel and result in meaningful actions, such as purchases or sign-ups.

Brand Building: Through consistent and value-driven email communications, brands can establish a strong online presence and build a loyal customer base.

As we delve into the depths of email marketing, we'll explore how to build an effective email marketing strategy, create compelling content, navigate the intricacies of automation and segmentation, adhere to legal considerations, measure campaign success, and ultimately, how beginners can embark on their journey to multiply sales and leads through this powerful marketing channel.

Building Your Email Marketing Strategy

A well-structured email marketing strategy is the cornerstone of successful campaigns that drive engagement and conversions. To maximize the impact of your email marketing efforts, you need a clear plan that outlines your goals, target audience, content approach, and tactics. Here's a step-by-step guide to building an effective email marketing strategy

Defining Your Target Audience for Email Marketing

One of the foundational steps in creating a successful email marketing campaign is defining your target audience. Understanding who your audience is, their needs, preferences, and behaviors, is essential for crafting relevant and engaging email content. Here's a comprehensive guide on how to define your target audience for effective email marketing:

1. Conduct Market Research:

Start by conducting thorough market research to gather insights about your industry, competitors, and customer demographics.

Identify trends, customer pain points, and gaps in the market that your products or services can address.

2. Develop Customer Personas:

Create detailed customer personas, which are fictional representations of your ideal customers.

Consider factors such as demographics (age, gender, location), psychographics (interests, values, lifestyle), and behavioral traits.

3. Analyze Your Existing Customers:

Study your current customer base to identify patterns and common characteristics.

Look for recurring traits among your most engaged and loyal customers.

4. Segment Your Audience:

Divide your audience into segments based on shared characteristics, interests, or behaviors.

Segmentation allows you to tailor your email content to specific groups, increasing relevance and engagement.

5. Identify Pain Points and Needs:

Understand the challenges, pain points, and needs your target audience faces.

Your email content should address these issues and provide solutions or valuable information.

6. Consider Buying Cycle Stages:

Recognize where your audience stands in the buying cycle: awareness, consideration, or decision.

Tailor your email content to guide them through the stages and provide the right information at the right time.

7. Utilize Social Media Insights:

Analyze your social media followers' engagement, interests, and interactions to gain insights into their preferences.

This data can provide valuable information about what content resonates with your audience.

8. Survey Your Audience:

Conduct surveys or feedback forms to directly gather information from your audience.

Ask questions about their preferences, challenges, and what type of content they would like to receive.

9. Monitor Analytics:

Use email marketing and website analytics to track user behavior and engagement.

Analyze metrics like open rates, click-through rates, and conversion rates to understand what resonates with your audience.

10. Stay Agile:

Continuously monitor and adapt your audience definition as your business and industry evolve.

Market trends, consumer preferences, and behaviors can change over time.

11. Test and Refine:

A/B test different email content and offers to see what performs best with different segments.

Use the results to refine your targeting and messaging strategies.

12. Avoid Assumptions:

Base your audience definition on data and insights rather than assumptions or stereotypes.

Don't assume that your audience is the same as your competitors' or that it hasn't changed over time.

13. Persona Example:

For example, if you're a fitness apparel brand, you might have personas like "Active Amanda," a 30-year-old yoga enthusiast, or "Gym-Goer Greg," a 25-year-old weightlifter.

Defining your target audience is a continuous process that requires ongoing research, analysis, and adaptation. By intimately understanding who your audience is and what they want, you can create email campaigns that resonate, drive engagement, and ultimately contribute to the success of your business.

Setting Clear Goals and Objectives for Email Marketing

Setting clear and measurable goals and objectives is a critical step in developing a successful email marketing strategy. Well-defined goals provide direction, focus, and a benchmark for evaluating the effectiveness of your campaigns. Here's how to set clear goals and objectives for your email marketing efforts:

1. Align with Business Objectives:

Start by aligning your email marketing goals with your overall business objectives. Your email campaigns should contribute to larger business goals such as increasing revenue, brand awareness, or customer retention.

2. Use the SMART Criteria:

Make your goals SMART: Specific, Measurable, Achievable, Relevant, and Time-bound.

Specific: Clearly state what you want to achieve.

Measurable: Define how you will measure success using specific metrics.

Achievable: Ensure your goals are realistic and attainable based on available resources.

Relevant: Ensure your goals are relevant to your business and marketing strategies.

Time-bound: Set a specific timeline for achieving your goals.

3. Choose Relevant Metrics:

Select key performance indicators (KPIs) that align with your goals. Common email marketing KPIs include:

Open Rate: The percentage of recipients who open your email.

Click-Through Rate (CTR): The percentage of recipients who click on a link in your email.

Conversion Rate: The percentage of recipients who complete a desired action.

Revenue Generated: The monetary value of conversions attributed to your email campaigns.

4. Define Email Campaign Objectives:

Specify the objectives for each email campaign. Are you trying to drive sales, increase website traffic, promote an event, or encourage social media engagement?

Each campaign's objectives should contribute to your larger email marketing goals.

5. Set Quantifiable Targets:

Set specific targets for each metric you're measuring. For example, aim for a 15% increase in open rates or a 20% increase in click-through rates over the next quarter.

6. Consider Customer Journey Stages:

Align your goals with different stages of the customer journey, such as awareness, consideration, and conversion.

Craft emails and objectives that guide recipients through each stage.

7. Prioritize Long-Term and Short-Term Goals:

Balance long-term objectives (e.g., building customer loyalty) with short-term goals (e.g., driving immediate sales).

Long-term goals create lasting impact, while short-term goals provide immediate results.

8. Review and Revise Regularly:

Regularly review your goals and objectives to ensure they remain relevant and aligned with business changes.

Make adjustments based on performance data and new insights.

9. Example:

Business Objective: Increase online sales by 20% in the next quarter.

SMART Goal: Achieve a 25% increase in click-through rate and a 15% increase in conversion rate for our promotional email campaign within two months.

Metrics: Click-Through Rate (CTR), Conversion Rate, Revenue Generated.

10. Celebrate Achievements:

Celebrate when you achieve your goals, and analyze what worked well.

Learn from both successes and failures to refine your future strategies.

Setting clear goals and objectives for your email marketing campaigns provides a roadmap for success. It helps you stay focused, measure progress, and continuously optimize your strategies to achieve better results over time.

Choosing an Email Marketing Platform

Selecting the right email marketing platform is crucial for executing effective campaigns, managing your subscriber list, and tracking performance. With numerous options available, it's important to choose a platform that aligns with your business needs and provides the features required for your email marketing success. Here's how to choose the best email marketing platform for your business:

1. Define Your Requirements:

Identify your specific needs and objectives for email marketing. Consider factors such as:

Size of your subscriber list.

Types of campaigns you plan to run (e.g., newsletters, promotions, automated sequences).

Level of automation you require.

Integration with other tools (e.g., e-commerce platforms, CRM systems).

2. Budget Considerations:

Determine how much you're willing to invest in an email marketing platform.

Compare pricing plans and features to find a solution that fits your budget.

3. Features and Functionality:

Look for features that match your needs, such as:

Email templates and customization options.

List management and segmentation capabilities.

Automation tools (e.g., autoresponders, drip campaigns).

A/B testing for optimizing campaigns.

Analytics and reporting.

Integration with other software you use (e.g., CRM, e-commerce platforms).

4. User-Friendly Interface:

Choose a platform with an intuitive and user-friendly interface.

The platform should be easy to navigate and use, even for those with limited technical skills.

5. Scalability:

Consider the platform's ability to scale as your business grows and your subscriber list expands.

Ensure it can accommodate your needs both now and in the future.

6. Deliverability and Security:

A good email marketing platform should prioritize deliverability, ensuring your emails land in recipients' inboxes rather than spam folders.

Look for security features to protect your data and subscribers' information.

7. Customer Support:

Choose a platform that offers reliable customer support, whether through email, live chat, or phone.

Timely assistance is important, especially if you encounter technical issues.

8. Integration Options:

If you use other software tools, ensure the email marketing platform integrates seamlessly with them.

Integration simplifies data management and improves efficiency.

9. Mobile Responsiveness:

Opt for a platform that supports mobile-responsive email design.

Many recipients open emails on mobile devices, so your emails should display properly on various screens.

10. Reputation and Reviews:

Research the platform's reputation and read user reviews to gauge user satisfaction and reliability.

Look for platforms with a positive track record.

11. Free Trials or Demos:

Take advantage of free trials or demos to test the platform's features and interface.

This hands-on experience can help you determine if it meets your needs.

12. Examples of Email Marketing Platforms:

Mailchimp: Offers a user-friendly interface, customizable templates, and automation features.

Constant Contact: Provides drag-and-drop editing, list segmentation, and reporting.

HubSpot: Offers marketing automation, CRM integration, and advanced reporting.

13. Consider Future Needs:

Think about your long-term email marketing goals. Will the platform accommodate your future needs as your strategies evolve?

14. Make an Informed Decision:

After researching and comparing platforms, choose the one that best aligns with your requirements, budget, and growth plans.

Choosing the right email marketing platform empowers you to create engaging campaigns, effectively manage your subscriber list, and track performance to achieve your goals. Take your time to evaluate options and select a platform that sets the foundation for successful email marketing efforts.

Creating an Effective Email List

A high-quality and engaged email list is the backbone of successful email marketing campaigns. Building and maintaining an effective email list ensures that your messages reach interested and receptive recipients. Here's how to create and grow an email list that drives engagement and conversions:

i. Start with Permission
ii. Use Sign-Up Forms
iii. Create Compelling Content
iv. Segment Your Audience
v. Leverage Landing Pages
vi. Run Contests and Giveaways
vii. Optimize Your Website for Conversion
viii. Use Social Media
ix. Attend Events and Webinars
x. Guest Blogging and Partnerships
xi. Offer Value
xii. Mobile-Friendly Experience
xiii. Use Pop-Up and Slide-In Forms
xiv. 14. Promote Referrals
xv. 15. Regularly Clean Your List

Remove inactive or bounced email addresses from your list to maintain a healthy list and deliverability rates.

Regular list cleaning improves open rates and engagement.

Creating an effective email list is a gradual process that requires ongoing effort and optimization. Focus on attracting subscribers who genuinely want to hear from you, and consistently provide value through your email content to keep them engaged over time.

Collecting Email Addresses

Collecting email addresses is a fundamental step in building your email marketing list. However, it's essential to ensure that you collect email addresses ethically and with permission. Here's how to collect email addresses effectively while maintaining best practices:

1. Use Sign-Up Forms on Your Website:

Place sign-up forms prominently on your website's homepage, landing pages, and blog posts.

Clearly communicate the benefits of subscribing, such as receiving exclusive content or special offers.

2. Offer Valuable Incentives:

Provide incentives for people to join your email list, such as discounts, ebooks, whitepapers, or access to exclusive webinars.

Make sure the incentive aligns with your target audience's interests.

3. Leverage Content Marketing:

Create high-quality content that addresses your audience's pain points or interests.

Use content upgrades, where visitors can exchange their email addresses for access to additional valuable content related to what they're reading.

4. Utilize Exit-Intent Pop-Ups:

Display pop-up forms when visitors are about to leave your website.

Offer a compelling reason for them to subscribe before exiting.

5. Segment and Personalize:

Use segmentation to offer relevant content and experiences based on user interests and behavior.

Personalized offers can encourage sign-ups.

6. Implement Social Media Campaigns:

Promote your email list on your social media platforms.

Run campaigns that encourage followers to subscribe in exchange for exclusive content.

7. Host Webinars and Events:

Organize webinars or virtual events and require participants to provide their email addresses to register.

Deliver valuable content during the event to encourage continued engagement.

8. Utilize Lead Magnets:

Create valuable resources like guides, templates, or checklists that your audience would find useful.

Offer these lead magnets in exchange for email addresses.

9. Attend Trade Shows and Events:

Collect email addresses from interested attendees at industry events, trade shows, and conferences.

Engage attendees with relevant content and offers.

10. Implement Referral Programs:

Encourage your current subscribers to refer friends, family, or colleagues to join your email list.

Offer rewards or incentives for successful referrals.

11. Guest Posting and Collaborations:

Contribute guest posts to blogs or platforms in your industry.

Include a call-to-action to subscribe to your email list for more valuable content.

12. Use QR Codes:

Include QR codes in print materials, such as brochures or business cards, that lead to your email sign-up form.

13. Run Online Contests and Giveaways:

Organize contests or giveaways that require participants to provide their email addresses to enter.

Ensure the prize aligns with your target audience's interests.

14. Transparency and Privacy:

Clearly communicate how you'll use subscribers' email addresses and that you respect their privacy.

Provide a link to your privacy policy to build trust.

15. Avoid Buying Email Lists:

Never buy email lists as it can harm your reputation and result in poor engagement.

Focus on building a list of engaged and interested subscribers.

16. Confirmation and Double Opt-In:

Implement a double opt-in process where subscribers confirm their subscription.

This ensures that subscribers genuinely want to receive your emails.

Remember, the key to collecting email addresses is to focus on quality over quantity. Engage with your subscribers authentically, provide value, and nurture the relationships you build through your email marketing campaigns.

Permission-Based Marketing

Permission-based marketing, also known as opt-in marketing, is a foundational principle in ethical and effective email marketing. It involves obtaining explicit permission from individuals before sending them marketing emails. This approach ensures that your recipients are genuinely interested in your content, leading to higher engagement rates, better deliverability, and a stronger brand reputation. Here's how to practice permission-based marketing in your email campaigns:

1. Obtain Explicit Consent:

Always ask for permission before adding someone to your email list. This can be through sign-up forms, checkboxes, or consent statements.

Use clear and specific language to explain what kind of emails they will receive and how often.

2. Use Double Opt-In:

Implement a double opt-in process where subscribers confirm their subscription by clicking a verification link in a confirmation email.

This additional step ensures that subscribers are genuinely interested and helps prevent spam complaints.

3. Avoid Purchased Lists:

Never buy or use email lists from third-party sources. These lists often contain uninterested or inactive recipients and can lead to deliverability issues and legal consequences.

4. Focus on Engagement:

Concentrate on engaging your existing subscribers through relevant and valuable content.

Engagement improves your sender reputation and keeps your list active and interested.

5. Provide Clear Unsubscribe Options:

Include a visible and easy-to-use unsubscribe link in every email.

Honoring unsubscribe requests promptly is not only a legal requirement (CAN-SPAM Act) but also builds trust.

6. Respect Privacy and Data Protection:

Clearly explain how you will use subscribers' data and respect their privacy rights.

Comply with data protection regulations such as GDPR (General Data Protection Regulation) and CCPA (California Consumer Privacy Act).

7. Segment and Personalize Content:

Use segmentation to send targeted content that aligns with subscribers' interests and preferences.

Personalized content encourages engagement and demonstrates that you value your subscribers' preferences.

8. Monitor Engagement Metrics:

Regularly track open rates, click-through rates, and conversion rates.

Analyze engagement metrics to gauge the effectiveness of your email campaigns and adjust your strategies as needed.

9. Provide Value Consistently:

Send valuable content that aligns with subscribers' expectations and interests.

Consistently delivering value maintains subscriber engagement and reduces the likelihood of unsubscribes.

10. Re-Engagement Campaigns:

If subscribers become inactive, implement re-engagement campaigns to reconnect with them.

Offer incentives, ask for feedback, or provide a compelling reason for them to remain on your list.

11. Stay Compliant with Regulations:

Familiarize yourself with email marketing regulations and comply with them.

Adhering to legal requirements builds trust and avoids legal issues.

12. Build Long-Term Relationships:

The goal of permission-based marketing is to establish and nurture long-term relationships with your audience.

Focus on building trust and delivering value to maintain subscriber engagement over time.

By following permission-based marketing practices, you ensure that your email marketing campaigns are welcomed by recipients, leading to improved engagement, better deliverability rates, and a positive brand image.

Segmentation and Personalization

Segmentation and personalization are two powerful strategies that can significantly enhance the effectiveness of your email marketing campaigns. By tailoring your messages to specific audience segments and delivering personalized content, you can increase engagement, relevance, and conversions. Here's how to effectively implement segmentation and personalization in your email marketing:

1. Segment Your Audience:

Divide your email list into smaller segments based on shared characteristics, behaviors, or preferences.

Common segmentation criteria include demographics, location, purchase history, engagement level, and interests.

2. Benefits of Segmentation:

Improved Relevance: Segmented emails are more relevant to recipients' interests and needs.

Higher Open and Click Rates: Relevant content leads to higher engagement rates.

Reduced Unsubscribes: Sending irrelevant content can lead to unsubscribes, which segmentation can help mitigate.

3. Types of Segmentation:

Demographic: Age, gender, location, etc.

Behavioral: Past purchases, website visits, engagement level.

Psychographic: Interests, values, lifestyle.

Purchase History: Frequency, product categories, average order value.

4. Personalize Content:

Use recipient data to personalize email content, including subject lines, salutations, and email copy.

Personalization can extend to recommending products, offering exclusive discounts, and acknowledging past interactions.

5. Dynamic Content:

Implement dynamic content blocks that change based on the recipient's characteristics or behavior.

Show product recommendations or offers tailored to each subscriber.

6. Behavioral Triggers:

Set up automated emails triggered by specific user actions, such as abandoned carts or product views.

These emails can prompt recipients to take the next step in the customer journey.

7. Lifecycle Stages:

Tailor your content to match where subscribers are in their customer journey (e.g., new subscribers, loyal customers, inactive users).

This ensures that your messages are relevant and resonate with each stage.

8. A/B Testing:

Test different approaches within your segments to identify what resonates best.

Experiment with subject lines, content, and calls-to-action to optimize your campaigns.

9. Testing and Optimization:

Continuously test and refine your segmentation strategies based on engagement and conversion data.

Adapt your segments as your audience's preferences evolve.

10. Automation:

Use automation tools to streamline personalized communication.

Set up drip campaigns that nurture leads with relevant content over time.

11. Data Accuracy:

Maintain accurate and up-to-date subscriber data to ensure effective segmentation.

Regularly clean and update your email list to remove invalid or outdated information.

12. Case Study:

For example, a clothing retailer could segment its audience by gender and purchase history. They could then personalize emails to male customers with recommendations for men's clothing based on past purchases, and similarly for female customers.

Implementing segmentation and personalization requires a deep understanding of your audience and their preferences. By delivering content that speaks directly to their needs, interests, and behaviors, you can build stronger connections, drive engagement, and achieve better results with your email campaigns.

Crafting Compelling Email Content

Creating compelling email content is essential for capturing your subscribers' attention, driving engagement, and ultimately achieving your email marketing goals. Whether you're sending newsletters, promotional offers, or educational content, the way you structure and deliver your message can significantly impact your campaign's success. Here's how to craft compelling email content:

Subject Lines that Grab Attention in Email Marketing

A captivating subject line is the key to getting your email opened and read. It's the first impression you make on your recipients, so crafting subject lines that grab attention is essential for the success of your email marketing campaigns. Here are strategies to create subject lines that entice recipients to open your emails:

1. Personalization:

Use the recipient's name in the subject line to create a sense of familiarity.

Personalization increases the likelihood of your email being opened.

2. Curiosity and Intrigue:

Pose a question or use a teaser to pique recipients' curiosity.

Encourage them to open the email to find out more.

3. Urgency and Scarcity:

Convey a sense of urgency or scarcity to encourage immediate action.

Phrases like "Limited Time Offer" or "Last Chance" can create a sense of urgency.

4. Benefit-Oriented Language:

Clearly communicate the benefit or value recipients will gain from opening the email.

Highlight how your email addresses their pain points or solves a problem.

5. Personalization and Location:

Incorporate location-based personalization to make the email feel relevant to the recipient's area.

Mentioning their city or region can increase open rates.

6. Emotion and Storytelling:

Evoke emotions or tell a short story in the subject line.

Emotional subject lines can resonate deeply and encourage engagement.

7. Use Numbers and Lists:

Numbers and lists attract attention and provide a clear expectation of what's inside the email.

For example, "5 Tips for Boosting Your Productivity."

8. Humor and Wit:

Inject humor or wit into your subject lines to stand out in recipients' inboxes.

Make sure the humor aligns with your brand personality.

9. Tease Exclusive Content:

Mention exclusive content or offers that recipients can only access by opening the email.

People are more likely to open emails for exclusive benefits.

10. Personal Achievements:

Acknowledge recipients' achievements or milestones in the subject line.

Celebrating them can create a positive emotional connection.

11. Use Emojis:

Emojis can add visual interest and personality to subject lines.

Use them sparingly and ensure they align with your brand tone.

12. Segment-Based Personalization:

Tailor subject lines based on segments and their specific interests or behaviors.

A relevant subject line increases open rates.

13. Keep it Short and Sweet:

Subject lines should be concise, around 4-7 words is ideal.

Short subject lines are more likely to be fully visible on mobile devices.

14. Avoid Spam Trigger Words:

Stay away from words that are commonly associated with spam emails.

Words like "free," "urgent," and excessive use of punctuation can trigger spam filters.

15. Use Teasers:

Provide a hint of what's inside without revealing everything.

Teasers can arouse curiosity and encourage opens.

Remember that subject lines should accurately reflect the content of your email to maintain trust and engagement. Experiment with different approaches, analyze performance metrics, and refine your subject line strategies to continuously improve your email open rates.

Designing Visually Appealing Emails

The visual design of your emails plays a critical role in capturing your audience's attention and conveying your message effectively. Well-designed emails not only look professional but also enhance the user experience, encourage engagement, and drive conversions. Here's how to design visually appealing emails:

1. Choose a Clean Layout:

Use a clean and organized layout that makes it easy for recipients to scan and understand the content.

Avoid clutter and prioritize hierarchy.

2. Mobile-Responsive Design:

Ensure your email design is responsive and adapts seamlessly to different screen sizes, especially mobile devices.

Most emails are opened on mobile, so a responsive design is crucial.

3. Consistent Branding:

Use your brand colors, fonts, and logo consistently in your email design.

Maintain a consistent visual identity across all touchpoints.

4. Eye-Catching Header:

Place a visually appealing header at the top of the email that reinforces your brand and message.

Use high-quality images or graphics that resonate with your audience.

5. Use White Space:

Incorporate ample white space to create a clean and uncluttered design.

White space improves readability and guides the recipient's focus.

6. Compelling Visuals:

Use relevant images, GIFs, or videos to enhance your email's visual appeal.

Visual content can convey information more effectively than text alone.

7. Clear Typography:

Choose readable fonts and sizes for your email copy.

Maintain consistency to ensure a cohesive design.

8. Call-to-Action (CTA) Design:

Make your CTAs stand out by using contrasting colors, larger fonts, or buttons.

Use action-oriented language to encourage clicks.

9. Use Bullet Points and Subheadings:

Break up your content with bullet points and subheadings to make it more scannable.

Subheadings help guide readers through the email's sections.

10. Simple Navigation:

If your email has multiple sections or content blocks, use clear navigation links.

Recipients should be able to easily jump to the content they're interested in.

11. Pre-Header Text:

Utilize the pre-header text (the text that appears after the subject line) to provide additional context or a preview of the email's content.

This can encourage recipients to open the email.

12. Social Sharing Buttons:

Include buttons or icons that allow recipients to easily share your email content on social media.

Social sharing can extend your reach beyond your email list.

13. Alt Text for Images:

Add alt text to your images for recipients who have images disabled in their email client.

Alt text provides context and ensures accessibility.

14. Test on Different Email Clients:

Preview and test your email design on various email clients and devices.

Ensure your design looks consistent and functions properly everywhere.

15. A/B Testing:

Test different design elements, such as color schemes, layout, and imagery, to identify what resonates best with your audience.

A/B testing helps optimize your design for engagement.

16. Clear Unsubscribe Option:

Include an easily accessible unsubscribe link as required by regulations.

This builds trust and ensures compliance.

Creating visually appealing emails involves a combination of design principles and an understanding of your audience's preferences. Prioritize readability, branding, and a user-friendly experience to create emails that not only look great but also effectively convey your message and drive action.

Writing Engaging and Relevant Content for Email Marketing

Compelling content is the heart of successful email marketing. To keep your subscribers engaged and motivated to take action, your email content must be relevant, valuable, and resonate with their needs and interests. Here's how to write engaging and relevant content for your email campaigns:

1. Understand Your Audience:

Develop a deep understanding of your target audience's demographics, preferences, pain points, and aspirations.

Tailor your content to address their specific needs and interests.

2. Craft Clear and Concise Copy

Write concise and scannable copy that gets to the point quickly.

Use short paragraphs, bullet points, and subheadings to break up the content.

3. Provide Value:

Offer valuable insights, tips, or solutions that your audience can benefit from.

Address their pain points and provide actionable advice.

4. Align with Email Goals:

Ensure that your content aligns with the goals of your email campaign.

If your goal is to promote a new product, focus on its benefits and unique features.

5. Use Attention-Grabbing Openers:

Start with an attention-grabbing hook or question in the opening lines.

Capture your recipients' curiosity right from the beginning.

6. Personalization:

Use personalization to address recipients by their first name and tailor content based on their preferences or past interactions.

Personalization creates a more intimate connection.

7. Storytelling:

Use storytelling techniques to make your content relatable and memorable.

Share anecdotes, case studies, or success stories that resonate with your audience.

8. Use Emotional Appeal:

Evoke emotions that align with your message and brand.

Emotional content tends to resonate deeply with recipients.

9. Solve Problems:

Offer solutions to common problems your audience faces.

Position your product or service as the solution.

10. Offer Exclusive Content:

Provide exclusive content that's only available to your email subscribers.

Exclusive offers encourage engagement and loyalty.

11. Create Scarcity or Urgency:

Use phrases like "Limited Time Offer" or "While Supplies Last" to create a sense of urgency.

Scarcity and urgency can drive action.

12. Use Conversational Tone:

Write in a conversational and relatable tone.

Avoid overly formal language to foster a genuine connection.

13. Use Visuals Wisely:

Include relevant images or visuals that enhance your message.

Visuals can convey information quickly and add visual interest.

14. Encourage Interaction:

Include interactive elements like polls, surveys, or quizzes.

Interaction boosts engagement and provides valuable insights.

15. Test and Optimize:

Regularly test different content approaches to see what resonates best with your audience.

Analyze performance metrics to refine your content strategy.

17. A/B Testing:

Experiment with different subject lines, content angles, and CTAs to find the most effective combinations.

A/B testing helps you fine-tune your content for better results.

18. Stay Consistent:

Maintain a consistent brand voice and messaging across all your email campaigns.

Consistency builds familiarity and trust.

By consistently delivering relevant and engaging content, you can foster a loyal and responsive subscriber base. Focus on providing value, addressing your audience's needs, and creating content that sparks genuine interest and action.

Call-to-Action (CTA) Strategies for Email Marketing

A well-crafted Call-to-Action (CTA) is a crucial element of your email marketing campaigns. It directs your recipients on what action to take next, whether it's making a purchase, signing up for an event, or exploring your website. Here are effective strategies for creating compelling CTAs in your email campaigns:

1. Be Clear and Action-Oriented:

Use clear and specific language that tells recipients exactly what action you want them to take.

Use action verbs like "Shop Now," "Download," "Register," or "Learn More."

2. Make It Stand Out:

Use contrasting colors, bold fonts, or buttons to make your CTA visually distinct.

Ensure it catches the recipient's attention immediately.

3. Placement Matters:

Place the CTA where it's easily visible, such as near the top of the email or following the main content.

Don't bury it at the bottom where it might be overlooked.

4. Keep It Short:

Keep your CTA concise and to the point, usually around 2-5 words.

Use concise language that conveys the action and value quickly.

5. Create a Sense of Urgency:

Use words like "Limited Time," "Last Chance," or "Hurry" to create urgency.

Urgent language can motivate recipients to take action sooner.

6. Convey Benefits:

Highlight the benefits or value recipients will gain from clicking the CTA.

Clearly communicate what's in it for them.

7. Personalize CTAs:

Tailor CTAs based on recipient behavior, preferences, or past interactions.

Personalized CTAs can feel more relevant and compelling.

8. Use First-Person Language:

Frame the CTA using first-person language to create a sense of ownership.

For example, "Get My Discount" instead of "Get Your Discount."

9. A/B Testing:

Test different variations of your CTA to see which one performs better.

Experiment with wording, colors, and placement to optimize results.

10. Limit Choices:

Focus on one primary CTA per email to avoid overwhelming recipients.

Too many options can lead to decision paralysis.

11. Ensure Mobile-Friendly Design:

Make sure your CTA is easily clickable on mobile devices.

Use a large enough button size for touch screens.

12. Above the Fold:

Place your CTA above the fold, where it's visible without scrolling.

This increases the chances of it being seen and clicked.

13. Use Negative Space:

Surround your CTA with white space to draw attention to it.

A clutter-free design makes your CTA more prominent.

14. Test Different Formats:

Experiment with different CTA formats, such as buttons, text links, or images.

Different formats can resonate differently with your audience.

15. Highlight Social Proof:

If applicable, use social proof near your CTA, such as mentioning the number of people who have already taken the desired action.

Social proof can boost credibility and encourage action.

16. Consistency with Landing Page:

Ensure that the CTA's promise aligns with the content of the landing page it leads to.

Consistency improves user experience and trust.

Creating effective CTAs involves a combination of persuasive language, strategic design, and a deep understanding of your audience's motivations. By implementing these strategies, you can encourage more recipients to take the desired actions and maximize the impact of your email marketing campaigns.

Automation and Segmentation in Email Marketing

Automation and segmentation are powerful techniques that can significantly enhance the efficiency and effectiveness of your email marketing efforts. They allow you to send targeted, timely, and relevant messages to your subscribers, leading to higher engagement, conversions, and overall campaign success.

Benefits of Automation:

Saves Time: Automating repetitive tasks frees up your time for strategic planning and creativity.

Consistency: Ensure timely and consistent communication with your subscribers.

Personalization: Deliver personalized messages at scale based on user behavior and preferences.

Lead Nurturing: Nurture leads through the customer journey with relevant content and timely follow-ups.

Improved ROI: Automation can lead to increased revenue and improved return on investment.

Here's how to leverage automation and segmentation in your email marketing strategy:

The Importance of Automation in Email Marketing

Automation is a game-changing strategy in email marketing that offers numerous benefits for marketers, from saving time to delivering more personalized and timely content. It allows you to streamline your processes, engage your audience effectively, and achieve better results. Here's why automation is crucial for successful email marketing:

1. Time Efficiency:

Automation eliminates the need for manual, repetitive tasks.

Marketers can focus on strategy, creativity, and analyzing campaign performance.

2. Consistency:

Automated emails are sent at predetermined times or triggered by specific events.

Maintains consistent communication with your audience, reducing the risk of oversight.

3. Personalization at Scale:

Automation allows you to deliver personalized content to different segments of your audience.

Tailor messages based on behavior, preferences, and demographics.

4. Increased Engagement:

Timely and relevant content delivered through automation leads to higher engagement rates.

Subscribers are more likely to open, click, and interact with content that speaks to their needs.

5. Nurturing Leads:

Automated drip campaigns nurture leads through the customer journey.

Gradually build relationships, educate prospects, and guide them towards conversion.

6. Targeted Messaging:

Automation enables precise targeting of specific customer segments.

Deliver content that matches their interests, location, behavior, and purchase history.

7. Data-Driven Insights:

Automation platforms provide valuable insights into recipient behavior.

Understand open rates, click-through rates, conversion rates, and more to refine your strategies.

8. Abandoned Cart Recovery:

Automatically send reminders to users who abandoned their shopping carts.

Recover potential lost sales and encourage users to complete their purchases.

9. Time Zones and Optimal Timing:

Automation allows you to send emails based on recipients' time zones.

Increases the likelihood of emails being opened at a convenient time for subscribers.

10. Customer Lifecycle Marketing:

Automate emails for different stages of the customer lifecycle.

Welcome new subscribers, celebrate anniversaries, and re-engage inactive customers.

11. Scalability:

Automation makes it possible to manage large email lists without manual effort.

Reach thousands of subscribers with personalized content simultaneously.

12. Cross-Selling and Upselling:

Automatically recommend related or complementary products based on previous purchases.

Increase revenue by encouraging customers to make additional purchases.

13. A/B Testing and Optimization:

Automate A/B testing to experiment with subject lines, content, and CTAs.

Optimize your campaigns for better results over time.

14. Cost-Effective:

Automation platforms offer various pricing tiers, making it accessible for businesses of all sizes.

The return on investment is typically high due to increased efficiency and engagement.

15. Enhances Customer Experience:

Personalized and timely emails enhance the overall customer experience.

Builds customer loyalty, satisfaction, and trust in your brand.

16. Multichannel Integration:

Many automation platforms integrate with other marketing channels, creating a unified customer experience.

Coordinate email marketing efforts with social media, content marketing, and more.

Automation allows you to deliver the right message to the right person at the right time, all while reducing manual effort. It enhances the overall effectiveness of your email marketing campaigns, helps you build stronger relationships with your audience, and ultimately drives better results for your business.

Setting Up Automated Email Campaigns

Automated email campaigns are a powerful way to engage your audience, nurture leads, and drive conversions without the need for constant manual intervention. Whether you're welcoming new subscribers, recovering abandoned carts, or delivering targeted content, here's how to set up effective automated email campaigns:

1. Define Your Goals:

Clearly define the goals and objectives of your automated campaign.

Are you aiming to educate, promote, or re-engage your audience?

2. Choose an Email Marketing Platform:

Select an email marketing platform that offers automation features.

Popular platforms include Mailchimp, HubSpot, ActiveCampaign, and ConvertKit.

3. Identify Target Segments:

Determine the segments of your audience that will receive the automated emails.

Segments can be based on demographics, behavior, interests, or lifecycle stage.

4. Map the Customer Journey:

Create a flowchart or sequence that outlines the emails recipients will receive at each stage of the journey.

Map out triggers, delays, and the content of each email.

5. Types of Automated Campaigns:

a. Welcome Series:

Send a series of emails to new subscribers, introducing your brand and offering value.

Nurture and establish a connection from the start.

b. Abandoned Cart Recovery:

Set up triggers to send automated reminders to users who left items in their cart.

Encourage them to complete their purchase with incentives.

c. Drip Campaigns:

Create a series of emails that provide value over time.

Nurture leads, educate subscribers, and move them through the sales funnel.

d. Birthday or Anniversary Emails:

Send personalized emails to subscribers on their special occasions.

Offer discounts or special gifts as a token of appreciation.

e. Re-engagement Campaigns:

Identify inactive subscribers and automate re-engagement emails.

Encourage them to reconnect with your brand.

6. Create Compelling Content:

Craft engaging and relevant content for each email in the sequence.

Personalize the content based on the segment and goal of the campaign.

7. Set Triggers and Delays:

Define the triggers that initiate each email in the sequence.

Triggers can be actions like subscribing, clicking a link, or abandoning a cart.

Set appropriate delays between emails to avoid overwhelming recipients.

8. Design Email Templates:

Design visually appealing email templates that match your brand identity.

Ensure your templates are mobile-responsive for optimal viewing on different devices.

9. Craft Engaging Subject Lines:

Create subject lines that grab attention and encourage opens.

Test different subject lines to optimize open rates.

10. Configure Automation Rules:

Use your email marketing platform's automation features to set up the campaign.

Define the rules and conditions for each email to be sent.

11. Test and Review:

Test the entire automation sequence before launching.

Ensure that emails are being triggered correctly and that the content appears as intended.

12. Monitor and Analyze:

Once the campaign is live, monitor its performance.

Track open rates, click-through rates, and conversion rates.

13. Optimize and Iterate:

Analyze the data to identify areas for improvement.

Adjust your campaign based on what's working and what's not.

14. Maintain Relevance:

Regularly review and update your automated campaigns to ensure the content remains relevant and effective.

Automated email campaigns save you time while delivering targeted, relevant content to your audience. By setting up well-planned campaigns, you can nurture leads, increase engagement, and achieve your email marketing goals more efficiently.

Segmentation for Personalization in Email Marketing

Segmentation is a key strategy that enables you to tailor your email marketing messages to specific groups within your audience. By dividing your subscriber list into segments based on shared characteristics, behaviors, or preferences, you can deliver more personalized and relevant content. Here's how to use segmentation effectively for personalization in email marketing:

1. Understand Your Audience:

Gather data and insights about your subscribers' demographics, behavior, preferences, and interests.

Use this information to create segments that reflect different aspects of your audience.

2. Types of Segmentation:

a. Demographic Segmentation:

Divide your audience based on age, gender, location, occupation, etc.

Tailor content to match the preferences of different demographic groups.

b. Behavioral Segmentation:

Segment based on how subscribers interact with your emails, website, and products.

Categories can include engaged, inactive, frequent buyers, and more.

c. Psychographic Segmentation:

Group subscribers by their lifestyle, values, interests, hobbies, and attitudes.

Send content that resonates with their unique psychographic characteristics.

d. Lifecycle Stage Segmentation:

Segment based on where subscribers are in their customer journey.

Tailor content to match their stage, whether they're new leads or loyal customers.

e. Purchase History Segmentation:

Segment based on past purchase behavior and preferences.

Recommend complementary products or personalized offers.

3. Benefits of Segmentation:

a. Improved Relevance:

Deliver content that directly addresses the needs and interests of each segment.

Subscribers are more likely to engage with content that's relevant to them.

b. Higher Engagement Rates:

Segmented emails generally have higher open and click-through rates.

Personalized content captures attention and encourages interaction.

c. Better Conversion Rates:

Relevant and personalized content increases the likelihood of conversions.

Subscribers are more likely to take action when the message aligns with their needs.

d. Reduced Unsubscribes:

Sending relevant content reduces the likelihood of subscribers unsubscribing.

When recipients find value in your emails, they're more likely to stay subscribed.

4. Creating Segments:

a. Use Data Analytics:

Leverage your email marketing platform's analytics to gain insights into subscriber behavior.

Identify patterns that can help you define segments.

b. Survey Subscribers:

Use surveys to gather information about subscribers' preferences and interests.

Use survey data to create more accurate segments.

c. Monitor Purchase Behavior:

Track what products or categories subscribers are interested in or have purchased.

Tailor content and offers based on their preferences.

d. Incorporate Behavioral Triggers:

Set up automation triggers based on specific actions, like clicks or downloads.

Use triggers to deliver relevant content or follow-ups.

5. Personalize Content:

a. Subject Lines and Introductions:

Use personalization tokens to insert recipients' names in subject lines and introductions.

Adds a personal touch and grabs attention.

b. Product Recommendations:

Include personalized product recommendations based on past purchase behavior.

Show subscribers items they're likely to be interested in.

c. Dynamic Content:

Use dynamic content blocks to show different content to different segments within the same email.

Deliver a more personalized experience for each subscriber.

d. Exclusive Offers:

Send exclusive offers or discounts tailored to each segment's preferences.

Increases the likelihood of conversion.

6. Test and Optimize:

A/B test different approaches within your segments to find what resonates best.

Analyze performance metrics to optimize your segmentation strategy.

Segmentation allows you to deliver personalized experiences to your subscribers, increasing engagement and driving better results. By understanding your audience and tailoring your content to their specific needs, you can create a more meaningful and effective email marketing strategy.

Drip Email Campaigns: Nurturing Leads and Building Relationships

Drip email campaigns, also known as drip marketing or automated email series, are a series of pre-scheduled, automated emails sent to subscribers over a period of time. These campaigns are designed to nurture leads, provide value, and guide recipients through the customer journey. Drip campaigns are a powerful tool in email marketing, allowing you to build relationships and drive conversions. Here's how to create effective drip email campaigns:

1. Define Your Goal:

Determine the goal of your drip campaign. Are you educating, onboarding, upselling, or re-engaging?

Clear goals help shape the content and structure of your campaign.

2. Map Out the Customer Journey:

Create a flowchart or sequence that outlines the emails recipients will receive at different stages.

Map out triggers, delays, and content for each email in the series.

3. Choose Your Email Marketing Platform:

Select an email marketing platform that offers automation capabilities for drip campaigns.

Popular platforms include Mailchimp, HubSpot, ActiveCampaign, and ConvertKit.

4. Segment Your Audience:

Divide your subscriber list into segments based on demographics, behavior, interests, or lifecycle stage.

Segmentation ensures that your drip campaign content is relevant to each group.

5. Craft Compelling Content:

Create engaging and valuable content for each email in the series.

Offer insights, tips, resources, or exclusive offers that align with the campaign's goal.

6. Set Triggers and Delays:

Determine the triggers that initiate each email in the sequence.

Triggers can be actions like subscribing, downloading a resource, or making a purchase.

Set appropriate time delays between emails to provide a steady, paced experience.

7. Personalize Where Possible:

Use personalization tokens to insert recipients' names and other personalized details.

Personalization creates a more individualized and engaging experience.

8. Call-to-Action (CTA):

Each email should have a clear and relevant CTA.

Guide recipients toward the next step in the journey, whether it's reading a blog post or making a purchase.

9. Monitor Performance:

Track key metrics such as open rates, click-through rates, and conversion rates.

Monitor how recipients are engaging with the emails in your drip campaign.

10. Optimize and Iterate:

Analyze the data to identify areas for improvement.

Optimize your campaign based on what's resonating and what's not.

11. Examples of Drip Campaigns:

a. Welcome Series:

Send a series of emails to new subscribers, introducing your brand, offering resources, and nurturing the relationship.

b. Onboarding Series:

Help new customers get started with your product or service through a series of educational emails.

c. Lead Nurturing Series:

Educate leads with relevant content over time, guiding them toward a purchase decision.

d. Abandoned Cart Series:

Remind users who abandoned their carts about their unpurchased items, offering incentives to complete the purchase.

e. Re-engagement Series:

Re-engage inactive subscribers with targeted content and offers to reignite their interest.

f. Upsell/Cross-Sell Series:

Recommend complementary or upgraded products to existing customers based on their purchase history.

12. Benefits of Drip Campaigns:

a. Nurture Relationships:

Build rapport with subscribers by providing value and relevant content over time.

Establish trust and credibility.

b. Guide the Customer Journey:

Drip campaigns guide leads through the stages of the customer journey, from awareness to conversion.

c. Automation Efficiency:

Automating the process saves time and ensures consistent communication.

Focus on other aspects of your marketing strategy.

d. Better Conversions:

Nurtured leads are more likely to convert, as they've received targeted information and become more familiar with your brand.

e. Higher Engagement:

Engaging content keeps recipients interested and encourages them to interact with your emails.

Drip email campaigns are a powerful way to nurture leads, educate customers, and build long-lasting relationships. By crafting relevant content and using automation strategically, you can guide your audience through their journey and drive meaningful interactions and conversions.

]

Avoiding Common Email Marketing Mistakes

Email marketing is a valuable tool that can help businesses connect with their audience, nurture leads, and drive conversions. However, just like any marketing strategy, there are pitfalls that can hinder your success if not properly managed. Avoiding common email marketing mistakes is essential to ensure that your campaigns deliver the desired results and maintain a positive reputation. In this section, we'll explore some of the most frequent email marketing mistakes that businesses make and provide insights on how to steer clear of them. By understanding these pitfalls and implementing best practices, you can create more effective and impactful email marketing campaigns that engage your audience and achieve your goals.

Overcoming Spam Filters in Email Marketing

One of the challenges in email marketing is ensuring that your messages reach your subscribers' inboxes and don't get flagged as spam. Spam filters are designed to protect recipients from unsolicited and potentially harmful emails, but they can sometimes catch legitimate emails as well. Overcoming spam filters is crucial to ensure that your carefully crafted campaigns reach their intended audience. Here's how to navigate spam filters effectively:

1. Build a Quality Email List:

Start with a clean and well-maintained email list.

Avoid purchasing or using outdated lists, as they can lead to high bounce rates and trigger spam filters.

2. Use Permission-Based Marketing:

Send emails only to subscribers who have explicitly given you permission to contact them.

Implement a double opt-in process to verify subscribers' intent.

3. Avoid Spam Trigger Words:

Certain words and phrases can trigger spam filters.

Avoid using words like "free," "guarantee," "buy now," and excessive use of exclamation points.

4. Optimize Sender Information:

Use a recognizable sender name and email address.

Consistency in sender information builds trust and reduces the likelihood of being flagged as spam.

5. Craft Relevant and Valuable Content:

Deliver content that is relevant and valuable to your subscribers.

Avoid overly promotional language and focus on providing useful information.

6. Balance Text and Images:

Avoid using too many images in your emails.

Include a good balance of text and images to avoid triggering spam filters.

7. Use a Responsive Design:

Ensure that your emails are mobile-responsive.

Mobile-friendly emails are favored by both subscribers and spam filters.

8. Authenticate Your Emails:

Implement authentication protocols like SPF (Sender Policy Framework) and DKIM (DomainKeys Identified Mail).

These protocols help verify the legitimacy of your emails and improve deliverability.

9. Monitor Engagement Metrics:

Pay attention to engagement metrics like open rates, click-through rates, and reply rates.

Positive engagement signals to inbox providers that your emails are wanted by recipients.

10. Provide an Unsubscribe Option:

Make it easy for recipients to unsubscribe from your emails.

Including an unsubscribe link is not only a best practice but also a requirement under anti-spam regulations.

11. Segment Your Email List:

Segment your list based on subscriber behavior and preferences.

Sending targeted content reduces the chances of being marked as spam.

12. Test and Monitor Deliverability:

Use deliverability testing tools to check how your emails perform with different ISPs.

Regularly monitor your deliverability and take action if you notice any issues.

13. Avoid Misleading Subject Lines:

Craft subject lines that accurately represent the content of your email.

Misleading subject lines can lead to higher unsubscribe rates and spam reports.

14. Maintain a Healthy Sending Reputation:

Avoid sending large volumes of emails in a short period.

Maintain a consistent sending frequency to build a positive sending reputation.

Overcoming spam filters requires a combination of best practices, technical measures, and a deep understanding of your subscribers' preferences. By adhering to these guidelines, you can increase the chances of your emails landing in recipients' inboxes, ensuring that your messages are seen and engaged with by your target audience..

Optimizing Frequency and Timing of Email Campaigns

The frequency and timing of your email campaigns play a crucial role in the success of your email marketing strategy. Sending emails too often or at the wrong times can lead to subscriber fatigue and decreased engagement. On the other hand, sending emails strategically can maximize open rates, click-through rates, and overall campaign effectiveness. Here's how to optimize the frequency and timing of your email campaigns:

1. Understand Your Audience:

Know your audience's preferences, behavior, and time zones.

Tailor your email schedule to match when they're most likely to be active.

2. Consistency is Key:

Maintain a consistent sending schedule to set expectations for your subscribers.

Whether it's daily, weekly, or monthly, consistency helps build anticipation.

3. Test and Analyze:

Experiment with different sending frequencies and timing.

Use A/B testing to identify what works best for your specific audience.

4. Consider Audience Segmentation:

Different segments of your audience might prefer different sending frequencies and times.

Segment your list based on behavior and preferences to tailor your approach.

5. Avoid Overwhelming Subscribers:

Be mindful of sending too many emails in a short period.

Too many emails can lead to unsubscribes and decreased engagement.

6. Optimal Sending Times:

Send emails during times when your audience is most likely to check their inbox.

Generally, mid-week mornings and early afternoons tend to be effective.

7. Time Zone Considerations:

If your subscribers are spread across different time zones, consider segmenting by location.

Use email marketing platforms that allow you to send emails based on recipients' time zones.

8. Weekday vs. Weekend:

Experiment with sending emails on both weekdays and weekends.

Depending on your audience and industry, weekends might yield higher engagement.

9. Behavioral Triggers:

Use automation to send emails triggered by specific subscriber actions.

For example, send a welcome email immediately after someone subscribes.

10. Watch Engagement Metrics:

Monitor open rates, click-through rates, and conversion rates.

Adjust your sending frequency and timing based on these metrics.

11. Balance Content and Promotion:

Maintain a balance between content-driven and promotional emails.

Regularly sending value-added content keeps subscribers engaged.

12. Avoid Sending During Holidays:

During holidays and peak vacation times, people may not be checking their emails as frequently.

Consider adjusting your sending schedule during these periods.

13. Consider Industry Norms:

Research your industry's typical email sending practices.

This can provide insights into what's effective for your specific audience.

14. Unsubscribe and Feedback:

Monitor unsubscribe rates and gather feedback from subscribers.

If you notice an increase in unsubscribes, it might be a sign to adjust your frequency.

15. Adapt and Optimize:

Continuously analyze the performance of your email campaigns.

Adapt your frequency and timing based on subscriber behavior and engagement.

Finding the right balance between email frequency and timing requires careful consideration and ongoing optimization. By understanding your audience's preferences, testing different strategies, and analyzing engagement metrics, you can create a well-timed and well-received email marketing strategy that maximizes the impact of your campaigns.

A/B Testing for Email Marketing Optimization

A/B testing, also known as split testing, is a powerful technique that allows you to compare different versions of your email campaigns to determine which one performs better. By systematically testing various elements, you can optimize your email marketing strategy and improve key metrics like open rates, click-through rates, and conversions. Here's how to effectively implement A/B testing for email marketing:

1. Define Your Goal:

Determine the specific goal you want to achieve with the A/B test.

Whether it's improving open rates, click-through rates, conversions, or another metric, a clear goal guides your testing.

2. Choose a Variable to Test:

Identify the element you want to test. This could be the subject line, sender name, email content, CTA, layout, or any other aspect.

3. Create Variations:

Create two versions of the email, each with a single difference in the chosen variable.

Keep all other elements consistent between the two versions to accurately measure the impact of the tested variable.

4. Randomly Segment Your Audience:

Split your email list into two equal and randomized segments.

Send each version of the email to one of the segments.

5. Test Elements to Consider:

a. Subject Line:

Test different subject lines to see which one leads to higher open rates.

Experiment with personalization, length, urgency, and curiosity.

b. Sender Name:

Test using a personal name vs. your brand name as the sender.

Different sender names can impact open rates.

c. Email Content:

Test variations in the content, messaging, and format of the email.

Try different writing styles, imagery, and placement of key elements.

d. Call-to-Action (CTA):

Test different wording, colors, placement, and size of the CTA button.

Experiment with direct vs. subtle CTAs.

e. Visual Elements:

Test the impact of using different images, graphics, or videos.

Visual elements can greatly influence engagement.

6. Monitor and Compare Results:

Track the performance metrics of both versions of the email.

Compare open rates, click-through rates, conversions, and other relevant data.

7. Choose the Winner:

Identify the version that outperforms the other in achieving your goal.

The winning version becomes your optimized email for that specific element.

8. Implement Learnings:

Apply the insights gained from the A/B test to your future email campaigns.

Continuously refine your strategy based on successful test outcomes.

9. Iterate and Test Again:

A/B testing is an ongoing process. Continuously test new variables and ideas to optimize your campaigns further.

10. Sample Size and Statistical Significance:

Ensure that your sample size is large enough for meaningful results.

Use statistical tools to determine if the results are statistically significant.

11. Avoid Multivariate Testing:

Stick to testing one variable at a time to isolate the impact of that specific element.

Multivariate testing can make it difficult to attribute changes to individual elements.

A/B testing empowers you to make data-driven decisions and refine your email marketing strategy over time. By systematically testing different elements and analyzing the results, you can optimize your campaigns for better performance and engagement, ultimately driving improved outcomes from your email marketing efforts.

Compliance and Legal Considerations in Email Marketing

Email marketing is a powerful tool for building relationships, engaging with customers, and driving business growth. However, with the benefits come responsibilities, particularly in ensuring that your email marketing campaigns comply with relevant laws and regulations. Compliance and legal considerations play a significant role in maintaining your brand's reputation, protecting user privacy, and avoiding potential legal issues. In this section, we will explore the essential compliance and legal aspects you need to be aware of when conducting email marketing campaigns. By understanding and adhering to these regulations, you can ensure that your email marketing efforts are not only effective but also ethical and lawful.

Navigating CAN-SPAM Act and GDPR in Email Marketing

Two critical regulations that impact email marketing are the CAN-SPAM Act and the General Data Protection Regulation (GDPR). These regulations are designed to protect consumers' privacy and ensure ethical practices in digital communications. Understanding and adhering to the requirements of these regulations is essential for maintaining compliance, building trust with your audience, and avoiding legal repercussions. Let's explore the CAN-SPAM Act and GDPR and how they influence your email marketing strategy:

CAN-SPAM Act:

1. Overview:

The CAN-SPAM Act (Controlling the Assault of Non-Solicited Pornography And Marketing Act) is a U.S. law that sets the rules for commercial email communication.

It applies to all commercial emails, regardless of whether they are promotional or transactional.

2. Key Requirements:

a. Opt-Out Mechanism:

You must provide a clear and visible way for recipients to opt out of receiving future emails.

Once a recipient opts out, you have 10 business days to stop sending them emails.

b. Accurate Header Information:

Your "From," "To," "Reply-To," and routing information must accurately identify the sender.

Misleading header information is prohibited.

c. Subject Line Transparency:

The subject line must accurately reflect the content of the email.

Deceptive subject lines are not allowed.

d. Physical Address:

Your emails must include a valid physical postal address for your business.

This address can be a street address or a P.O. box.

e. Identification of Commercial Messages:

Clearly indicate that your email is a commercial message.

Recipients should know that the email is an advertisement.

3. Consent Requirements:

CAN-SPAM doesn't require explicit consent for sending marketing emails.

However, obtaining permission from recipients is good practice and can help maintain engagement and reputation.

General Data Protection Regulation (GDPR):

1. Overview:

GDPR is a European Union regulation that governs the processing of personal data of EU citizens.

It applies to businesses worldwide that process personal data of EU residents.

2. Key Principles:

a. Lawful Basis for Processing:

You must have a lawful basis for processing personal data.

Consent is one lawful basis, but there are others, such as contractual necessity or legitimate interests.

b. Explicit Consent for Marketing:

Explicit, informed consent is required for sending marketing emails.

Pre-checked boxes or assumed consent are not allowed.

c. Right to Access and Erasure:

Recipients have the right to access their data and request its deletion.

You must provide mechanisms for users to exercise these rights.

d. Data Protection Officer (DPO):

Appoint a Data Protection Officer if your organization processes large amounts of personal data or sensitive data.

e. Cross-Border Data Transfer:

Personal data can only be transferred to countries with adequate data protection standards.

3. Data Processing Agreements:

When using third-party email marketing platforms, ensure you have a data processing agreement in place.

4. Breach Notification:

If there's a data breach, you must notify authorities and affected individuals within 72 hours.

Both the CAN-SPAM Act and GDPR aim to protect user privacy and ensure transparent, ethical, and lawful communication practices. While the CAN-SPAM Act focuses on commercial emails and is applicable primarily in the U.S., GDPR has a broader scope and affects businesses worldwide that interact with EU citizens. Adhering to these regulations is essential for maintaining a positive reputation, building trust with your audience, and avoiding legal complications in your email marketing endeavors.

Ensuring Privacy and Data Protection in Email Marketing

Privacy and data protection are fundamental aspects of ethical and effective email marketing. As the digital landscape evolves and concerns about personal data grow, ensuring the privacy and security of your subscribers' information is paramount. By implementing robust data protection measures and transparent practices, you can build trust, maintain compliance with regulations, and safeguard both your subscribers and your brand. Here's how to ensure privacy and data protection in your email marketing campaigns:

1. Obtain Informed Consent:

Only send emails to recipients who have explicitly opted in to receive communications.

Implement a clear and unambiguous opt-in process that explains what recipients are signing up for.

2. Transparency in Data Collection:

Clearly state why you're collecting data and how it will be used.

Provide a link to your privacy policy that outlines data usage, sharing, and retention practices.

3. Secure Data Storage:

Safeguard subscriber data through robust security measures.

Use encryption to protect sensitive information both during transmission and storage.

4. Permission-Based Marketing:

Avoid purchasing or using third-party lists without clear opt-in documentation.

Focus on building your own opt-in list through ethical means.

5. Privacy Policy and Terms of Use:

Maintain an up-to-date and comprehensive privacy policy that outlines your data handling practices.

Ensure your terms of use are transparent and easily accessible.

6. Data Minimization:

Collect only the data you need for your email marketing purposes.

Minimize the amount of personal information you request from subscribers.

7. Opt-Out Mechanism:

Provide a clear and easy way for subscribers to opt out of receiving emails.

Honor unsubscribe requests promptly and without hassle.

8. Secure Third-Party Services:

If you're using third-party email marketing platforms, ensure they adhere to stringent data protection standards.

Choose platforms that comply with relevant regulations and provide data protection agreements.

9. Regular Data Audits:

Periodically review your subscriber list to ensure it's accurate and up to date.

Remove inactive or disengaged subscribers to improve deliverability and engagement.

10. Data Access Requests:

Be prepared to respond to requests from subscribers to access or delete their data.

Have a process in place to handle these requests efficiently.

11. Training and Awareness:

Train your team on data protection principles and best practices.

Ensure everyone involved in email marketing understands their responsibilities.

12. Monitoring and Incident Response:

Regularly monitor your email marketing practices and data processing activities.

Have a plan in place to respond to data breaches or security incidents.

13. Compliance with Regulations:

Stay up to date with relevant regulations such as GDPR, CAN-SPAM Act, and others that apply to your audience.

14. Cross-Border Data Transfers:

If you're transferring data across borders, ensure compliance with data protection laws in both the source and destination countries.

15. Respect User Choices:

If subscribers opt out or request data removal, honor their choices promptly.

Show respect for their preferences and privacy.

Prioritizing privacy and data protection not only complies with legal requirements but also builds a positive reputation and long-lasting relationships with your subscribers. By implementing these practices, you demonstrate your commitment to ethical email marketing and contribute to a safer and more trusted online environment.

Measuring and Analyzing Email Campaigns

Effective email marketing doesn't stop at sending out well-crafted emails; it involves continuously assessing the performance of your campaigns to ensure they align with your goals and yield the desired results. Measuring and analyzing email campaigns is a crucial step in optimizing your strategy, improving engagement, and achieving higher conversion rates. In this section, we'll delve into the importance of tracking key metrics, understanding the analytics tools at your disposal, and using data-driven insights to refine your email marketing approach. By mastering the art of measurement and analysis, you can make informed decisions that drive the success of your email campaigns.

Key Metrics to Track in Email Marketing Campaigns

Tracking key metrics is essential for evaluating the effectiveness of your email marketing campaigns. These metrics provide insights into how well your emails are performing, where improvements can be made, and whether you're meeting your goals. By understanding and analyzing these metrics, you can optimize your strategy and achieve better results. Here are the key metrics you should track in your email marketing campaigns:

1. Open Rate:

The open rate measures the percentage of recipients who opened your email.

A high open rate indicates that your subject line and sender information were compelling.

2. Click-Through Rate (CTR):

The CTR measures the percentage of recipients who clicked on a link within your email.

It reflects the effectiveness of your content and calls-to-action (CTAs).

3. Conversion Rate:

The conversion rate measures the percentage of recipients who completed the desired action, such as making a purchase or signing up.

It helps you gauge the effectiveness of your emails in driving actual results.

4. Bounce Rate:

The bounce rate measures the percentage of emails that couldn't be delivered to recipients' inboxes.

Bounces can be categorized as hard (permanent) or soft (temporary).

5. Unsubscribe Rate:

The unsubscribe rate measures the percentage of recipients who chose to unsubscribe after receiving your email.

A higher unsubscribe rate might indicate issues with email content or targeting.

6. Spam Complaint Rate:

The spam complaint rate measures the percentage of recipients who marked your email as spam.

A high spam complaint rate can harm your sender reputation and deliverability.

7. Engagement Rate:

The engagement rate considers multiple factors such as opens, clicks, and conversions to provide a holistic view of how well your email resonates with recipients.

8. Return on Investment (ROI):

ROI measures the financial impact of your email campaigns.

It helps assess whether your email marketing efforts are generating a positive return.

9. List Growth Rate:

The list growth rate measures how quickly your email list is growing.

It's important to track this to ensure a healthy and engaged subscriber base.

10. Device and Platform Usage:

Understanding which devices and platforms your subscribers use to open emails helps optimize your email design and responsiveness.

11. Engagement by Segment:

Track metrics for different segments of your audience to understand how each group is engaging with your content.

12. Time of Engagement:

Analyze when recipients are most likely to open and engage with your emails.

Timing your sends based on this data can improve open and click-through rates.

13. A/B Testing Results:

Track the results of A/B tests to understand which variations of your emails perform better.

14. Conversion Path:

Analyze the path subscribers take after clicking through your email.

Identify drop-off points to optimize the user journey.

15. Social Sharing and Forwarding:

Track how often recipients share your emails on social media or forward them to others.

This can help increase your email's reach and engagement.

16. Landing Page Performance:

If your email directs recipients to a landing page, track its performance in terms of conversion rates and user behavior.

17. Revenue Attribution:

For e-commerce businesses, track how much revenue can be attributed to specific email campaigns.

By regularly tracking these key metrics and interpreting their implications, you can gain a comprehensive understanding of your email marketing performance. These insights empower you to make informed decisions, identify areas for improvement, and refine your strategy for more successful email campaigns.

Using Analytics to Improve Email Campaigns

Analytics are a powerful tool that can provide valuable insights into the performance of your email marketing campaigns. By leveraging data and interpreting analytics effectively, you can identify areas of strength and opportunities for improvement. This data-driven approach enables you to optimize your campaigns, enhance engagement, and achieve better results. Here's how to use analytics to improve your email marketing campaigns:

1. Identify High-Performing Content:

Analyze which types of content, topics, and formats generate the highest engagement.

Use this information to tailor your content strategy and provide more of what resonates with your audience.

2. Learn from A/B Testing:

Review the results of A/B tests to determine which variations had a positive impact.

Apply successful elements from these tests to future campaigns.

3. Segment Analysis:

Examine how different segments of your audience respond to your emails.

Adjust your content and messaging based on the preferences of specific segments.

4. Engagement Time Analysis:

Determine when subscribers are most active and engaged with your emails.

Schedule your sends to coincide with these times for better open and click-through rates.

5. Conversion Path Analysis:

Analyze the path subscribers take after clicking on your emails.

Optimize your landing pages and user journey to maximize conversions.

6. Click Heatmaps:

Use click heatmaps to visualize where subscribers are clicking within your emails.

Optimize your email layout and design based on these patterns.

7. Subject Line Performance:

Analyze which subject lines led to higher open rates.

Apply successful techniques to future subject lines.

8. Conversion Attribution:

Track which emails or campaigns led to conversions and revenue.

Use this data to prioritize and replicate successful strategies.

9. Subscriber Behavior Insights:

Gain insights into how subscribers interact with your emails.

Identify patterns and preferences to enhance personalization.

10. Unsubscribe and Spam Complaint Analysis:

Monitor unsubscribe and spam complaint rates.

Adjust your content and frequency to reduce unsubscribes and complaints.

11. Device and Platform Analysis:

Understand which devices and platforms subscribers use to open emails.

Optimize your emails for a better user experience on these platforms.

12. Long-Term Trends:

Analyze performance trends over time to identify any seasonal or cyclical patterns.

Use this information to plan future campaigns strategically.

13. Data Cleaning and List Management:

Regularly clean your email list to remove inactive or unengaged subscribers.

A cleaner list improves deliverability and engagement metrics.

14. Benchmark Against Goals:

Compare your campaign metrics against your predefined goals.

Adjust your strategy based on whether you're meeting your objectives.

15. Continuous Iteration:

Use analytics as a continuous feedback loop for improvement.

Test new ideas, analyze the results, and refine your approach accordingly.

Remember that analytics should guide your decision-making process. Regularly review your campaign metrics, draw meaningful insights, and apply those insights to refine your email marketing strategy. By adopting a data-driven mindset, you can continually enhance your campaigns, foster better engagement, and drive more impactful results.

Tracking Return on Investment (ROI) in Email Marketing

Return on Investment (ROI) is a critical metric for evaluating the success of your email marketing campaigns. It measures the financial impact of your campaigns by comparing the revenue generated from your email marketing efforts to the costs involved. Calculating and analyzing ROI provides insights into the effectiveness of your campaigns and helps you allocate resources more efficiently. Here's how to track ROI in email marketing:

1. Define Campaign Goals:

Clearly define the goals of your email campaigns, whether it's generating sales, increasing website traffic, or driving sign-ups.

2. Gather Data:

Collect data on the revenue generated as a direct result of your email campaigns.

Track sales, leads, conversions, and other desired actions that can be attributed to your emails.

3. Calculate Costs:

Determine the costs associated with your email marketing efforts.

This can include expenses for software, email marketing platforms, content creation, design, and personnel.

4. Use Attribution Models:

Choose an attribution model to attribute revenue to specific email campaigns.

Common models include first touch, last touch, linear, and time decay attribution.

5. Calculate ROI:

Use the formula: ROI = (Net Revenue - Cost of Campaign) / Cost of Campaign * 100.

Net revenue is the revenue generated from the campaign minus any refunds, discounts, or associated costs.

6. Compare ROI to Goals:

Compare the calculated ROI to the goals you set for the campaign.

Assess whether the campaign delivered the expected returns.

7. Segment Analysis:

Analyze ROI by segment to understand which audience groups or segments are generating the highest returns.

Tailor your future campaigns based on this insight.

8. Lifetime Value (LTV):

Consider the lifetime value of customers acquired through email campaigns.

A high LTV can justify higher initial acquisition costs.

9. Compare ROI Across Campaigns:

Compare the ROI of different campaigns to identify which types of emails or strategies yield the best returns.

Use this information to allocate resources effectively.

10. Timeframes and Trends:

Analyze ROI trends over different timeframes (e.g., monthly, quarterly, annually).

Identify any seasonal or long-term patterns in your ROI data.

11. Factor in Customer Acquisition Costs:

Consider the costs associated with acquiring new customers through email campaigns.

Include costs like advertising, lead generation, and nurturing.

12. Monitoring Campaign Impact:

Track ROI beyond the initial conversion.

Consider the long-term impact of email campaigns on customer retention and repeat purchases.

13. Continuous Improvement:

Use ROI data to continually refine your email marketing strategy.

Focus resources on campaigns that consistently deliver positive returns.

14. Include Soft Benefits:

While ROI is primarily financial, also consider qualitative benefits like brand awareness, customer engagement, and improved customer relationships.

15. Document Insights:

Keep records of the insights gained from ROI analysis.

Apply these insights to future campaigns for ongoing improvement.

Tracking ROI in email marketing provides a clear understanding of the financial impact of your campaigns and enables you to make informed decisions about resource allocation and strategy refinement. By consistently monitoring and analyzing ROI, you can maximize the effectiveness of your email marketing efforts and drive better returns on your investment.

Beginner's Guide to Starting Email Marketing

Email marketing is a powerful tool for businesses of all sizes to connect with their audience, nurture relationships, and drive conversions. Whether you're a small startup, an independent creator, or a larger company, email marketing offers a cost-effective way to engage with your target audience and achieve your marketing goals. This beginner's guide is designed to provide you with a step-by-step overview of how to start your email marketing journey. From building your email list to crafting compelling campaigns and measuring success, this guide will equip you with the essential knowledge and strategies needed to launch effective email marketing campaigns and establish a strong online presence. Let's dive in and explore the foundational steps to get started with email marketing.

Building Your First Email List: A Beginner's Approach

Building an email list is the foundation of successful email marketing. Your email list consists of individuals who have shown interest in your brand, products, or content and have given you permission to communicate with them. As a beginner, it's important to start off on the right foot by ethically and effectively growing your email list. Here's a step-by-step guide to building your first email list:

1. Define Your Target Audience:

Determine who your ideal subscribers are.

Consider demographics, interests, and pain points to tailor your content to their needs.

2. Choose an Email Marketing Platform:

Select an email marketing platform that suits your needs and budget.

Popular options include Mailchimp, Constant Contact, and ConvertKit.

3. Create an Irresistible Lead Magnet:

Offer a valuable resource or incentive in exchange for subscribers' email addresses.

This could be an e-book, whitepaper, discount code, webinar, or exclusive content.

4. Design a Sign-Up Form:

Design a visually appealing sign-up form that aligns with your brand.

Place the form prominently on your website, blog, and social media profiles.

5. Implement Double Opt-In:

Use a double opt-in process to ensure that subscribers confirm their intention to join your list.

This helps reduce fake or incorrect email addresses and ensures high-quality leads.

6. Craft a Compelling Call-to-Action (CTA):

Your CTA should clearly convey the benefits of subscribing.

Use action-oriented language and highlight the value subscribers will receive.

7. Create Landing Pages:

Design dedicated landing pages for specific lead magnets.

Landing pages focus solely on the offer, increasing conversions.

8. Leverage Social Media:

Promote your lead magnets on social media platforms.

Use targeted ads to reach your desired audience.

9. Implement Content Upgrades:

Create content upgrades that complement your blog posts or content.

Offer additional valuable resources in exchange for email sign-ups.

10. Host Webinars or Workshops:

Host webinars or online workshops on topics relevant to your audience.

Collect email addresses from attendees during registration.

11. Collaborate and Guest Post:

Collaborate with influencers or industry experts for co-branded lead magnets.

Guest post on other platforms and include a link to your sign-up form.

12. Utilize Exit-Intent Popups:

Use exit-intent popups to capture the attention of visitors who are about to leave your site.

Offer a last-minute incentive to encourage them to subscribe.

13. Run Contests and Giveaways:

Organize contests or giveaways with email subscription as an entry requirement.

Promote the campaign on social media and other channels.

14. Offer Exclusive Content:

Promote the exclusivity of your email list.

Promise subscribers access to exclusive content, early releases, and special offers.

15. Regularly Engage Subscribers:

Once you have subscribers, engage them with valuable content.

Consistent engagement maintains interest and reduces unsubscribes.

Remember that building an email list is an ongoing process. Focus on quality over quantity, ensuring that your subscribers genuinely want to hear from you. As a beginner, take the time to build a strong foundation for your email list, and prioritize building relationships with your subscribers. This will set the stage for successful and impactful email marketing campaigns in the future.

Crafting Initial Email Content: A Beginner's Guide

Once you've built your email list, it's time to start engaging your subscribers with compelling content. The first emails you send are crucial for making a positive impression and establishing a strong connection. As a beginner, crafting effective initial email content might seem intimidating, but with the right approach, you can create emails that resonate with your audience and drive engagement. Here's a step-by-step guide to help you craft your initial email content:

1. Welcome Email:

Send a warm and friendly welcome email to new subscribers.

Express gratitude for their interest and briefly introduce your brand.

2. Set Expectations:

Clearly communicate the type and frequency of emails subscribers can expect.

Allow them to customize their email preferences.

3. Personalization:

Use the subscriber's name in the email to create a personalized touch.

Personalization increases engagement and makes subscribers feel valued.

4. Share Your Story:

Introduce yourself or your brand's story to humanize your communication.

Explain what you do and how you can provide value to your subscribers.

5. Provide Value:

Offer immediate value in your first email.

This could be in the form of a useful tip, a relevant resource, or exclusive content.

6. Call-to-Action (CTA):

Include a clear and relevant CTA that aligns with the purpose of the email.

This could be to explore your website, download a resource, or follow you on social media.

7. Visual Appeal:

Use a clean and visually appealing email design.

Include images that support your content and reinforce your brand identity.

8. Mobile Optimization:

Ensure your email is mobile-responsive.

A significant portion of subscribers will view emails on mobile devices.

9. Be Concise:

Keep your initial emails concise and to the point.

Grab subscribers' attention quickly and deliver value efficiently.

10. Avoid Over-Promotion:

While it's okay to promote your products or services, avoid excessive self-promotion.

Focus on building trust and providing value before making sales pitches.

11. Encourage Engagement:

Encourage subscribers to reply to your email with their thoughts or questions.

This helps foster a two-way communication channel.

12. Ask for Feedback:

Invite subscribers to provide feedback or suggestions.

This shows that you value their opinions and are open to improvement.

13. Use Conversational Language:

Write in a friendly and conversational tone.

Avoid jargon or overly formal language.

14. Proofread and Test:

Proofread your email to catch any spelling or grammatical errors.

Test your email across different email clients to ensure compatibility.

15. Segment and Target:

Segment your list and tailor your content to specific groups.

Relevant content increases engagement and resonates with subscribers.

16. Monitor Analytics:

Pay attention to open rates, click-through rates, and engagement metrics.

Analyze the performance of your initial emails to improve future campaigns.

Your initial email content sets the tone for your relationship with subscribers. As a beginner, focus on providing value, building trust, and establishing a connection. With practice, you'll develop a deeper understanding of your audience's preferences and refine your email content to create impactful and engaging campaigns.

Setting Up Basic Automated Email Campaigns: A Beginner's Guide

Automated email campaigns can significantly enhance your email marketing strategy by delivering relevant content to subscribers at the right time. As a beginner, automating your emails might seem complex, but with the right approach, you can create effective automated campaigns that nurture relationships and drive conversions. Here's a step-by-step guide to help you set up basic automated email campaigns:

1. Choose an Email Marketing Platform:

Select an email marketing platform that offers automation features.

Popular platforms like Mailchimp, ConvertKit, and ActiveCampaign provide user-friendly automation tools.

2. Define Your Campaign Goals:

Clearly define the objectives of your automated campaigns.

Common goals include welcoming new subscribers, nurturing leads, and re-engaging inactive subscribers.

3. Create Targeted Lists:

Segment your email list based on subscriber behavior, demographics, or preferences.

This allows you to send tailored content to specific segments.

4. Welcome Series:

Set up an automated welcome series for new subscribers.

Send a series of emails introducing your brand, offering value, and building a connection.

5. Abandoned Cart Emails:

If you're an e-commerce business, set up automated emails to remind users of items left in their cart.

Include compelling product images, descriptions, and a clear call-to-action.

6. Drip Campaigns:

Create drip campaigns that deliver a series of emails over a period of time.

Provide valuable content, tips, or educational resources that gradually nurture leads.

7. Re-Engagement Campaigns:

Set up automated campaigns to re-engage inactive subscribers.

Send emails with offers, exclusive content, or incentives to encourage them to become active again.

8. Birthday and Anniversary Emails:

Create automated emails to celebrate subscribers' birthdays or anniversaries.

Personalized messages and special offers can boost engagement.

9. Transactional Emails:

Set up automated transactional emails, such as order confirmations and shipping notifications.

These emails provide a seamless customer experience.

10. Test and Optimize:

Test your automated campaigns to ensure they work as intended.

Monitor metrics like open rates and click-through rates to identify areas for improvement.

11. Monitor and Adjust:

Regularly monitor the performance of your automated campaigns.

Adjust content, timing, and targeting based on subscriber engagement.

12. Personalize and Segment Content:

Tailor your automated emails based on subscriber preferences and behaviors.

Personalized content increases engagement and relevance.

13. Clear Call-to-Action (CTA):

Include a clear and actionable CTA in each automated email.

Guide subscribers toward the desired action, whether it's making a purchase or reading a blog post.

14. A/B Testing:

Experiment with different subject lines, content, and CTAs.

A/B testing helps you identify what resonates best with your audience.

15. Provide Value:

Focus on delivering value in your automated emails.

Solve problems, answer questions, and fulfill subscribers' needs.

As a beginner, start with these basic automated campaigns and gradually expand your automation strategy as you become more comfortable. Automated campaigns save time, increase efficiency, and deliver relevant content to your subscribers, ultimately leading to improved engagement and conversions.

Strategies to Multiply Sales and Leads

In the world of digital marketing, the ultimate goal is to drive tangible results for your business, and one of the most sought-after outcomes is increasing sales and leads. Achieving this requires a combination of effective strategies, targeted tactics, and a deep understanding of your audience. Whether you're just starting out or looking to refine your approach, this section explores a range of strategies that can help you multiply sales and leads through your marketing efforts. From optimizing your website to leveraging social media and embracing content marketing, these strategies are designed to empower you with the tools needed to accelerate your business growth and achieve your goals. Let's dive into the world of sales and lead multiplication strategies.

Creating Irresistible Offers: A Key to Generating Sales and Leads

An irresistible offer has the power to captivate your audience, drive engagement, and ultimately boost your sales and lead generation efforts. Crafting an offer that provides substantial value and resonates with your target audience is a skill that can significantly impact your business's success. Whether you're looking to attract new customers or entice existing ones, creating compelling offers is a strategy that can yield impressive results. Here's a comprehensive guide to help you create irresistible offers that effectively multiply sales and leads:

1. Understand Your Audience:

Start by gaining a deep understanding of your target audience's needs, pain points, and desires.

Tailor your offers to address their specific challenges and aspirations.

2. Offer Real Value:

Your offer should provide genuine value that addresses a pressing problem or fulfills a desire.

Ensure that the perceived benefit of the offer outweighs the effort or cost required from the audience.

3. Solve a Problem:

Craft offers that offer solutions to common problems your audience faces.

Highlight how your product or service can alleviate their pain points.

4. Create Scarcity:

Introduce a sense of urgency or scarcity to prompt quick action.

Limited-time offers or exclusive deals can drive immediate conversions.

5. Clearly Communicate Benefits:

Clearly outline the benefits and outcomes that recipients can expect from your offer.

Focus on how your offer can positively impact their lives or businesses.

6. Use Compelling Copy:

Craft persuasive and concise copy that emphasizes the value of your offer.

Highlight key benefits and use language that resonates with your audience.

7. Offer Multiple Choices:

Provide options within your offer to cater to different preferences or needs.

Different pricing tiers or package options can cater to a broader audience.

8. Bundle Products or Services:

Bundle related products or services together to offer a comprehensive solution.

Bundling can increase the perceived value and encourage larger purchases.

9. Include Bonuses:

Add complementary bonuses that enhance the value of the main offer.

Bonuses can sweeten the deal and make your offer more appealing.

10. Test and Refine:

A/B test different elements of your offer, such as pricing, messaging, and visuals.

Use data-driven insights to refine your offers based on what resonates best with your audience.

11. Leverage Social Proof:

Showcase testimonials, case studies, or reviews that demonstrate the effectiveness of your offer.

Social proof builds credibility and trust.

12. Optimize Landing Pages:

Design dedicated landing pages that focus solely on your offer.

Keep the messaging consistent and remove distractions that could divert attention.

13. Clear Call-to-Action (CTA):

Use a clear and compelling CTA that guides users to take action.

The CTA should reflect the desired outcome, whether it's making a purchase or signing up.

14. Measure and Adjust:

Monitor the performance of your offers using relevant metrics like conversion rates.

Analyze results and adjust your strategy based on what's working best.

15. Provide a Money-Back Guarantee:

Offer a risk-free guarantee to instill confidence in potential customers.

A money-back guarantee reduces perceived risk and encourages conversions.

Creating irresistible offers requires a deep understanding of your audience, a commitment to providing value, and effective communication. By following these strategies, you can craft offers that capture attention, drive action, and multiply both sales and leads, contributing to the growth and success of your business.

Upselling and Cross-Selling through Emails: Boosting Revenue and Customer Value

Upselling and cross-selling are powerful techniques that can significantly increase your revenue by maximizing the value of each customer interaction. These strategies involve offering complementary products or encouraging customers to upgrade to higher-priced options. When executed effectively through email marketing, upselling and cross-selling not only boost sales but also enhance customer satisfaction and loyalty. In this guide, we'll explore how to leverage upselling and cross-selling through emails to multiply your sales and customer lifetime value:

1. Understand Customer Behavior:

Study your customers' purchasing behavior and preferences.

Identify patterns that suggest opportunities for upselling and cross-selling.

2. Segment Your Email List:

Segment your email list based on customer preferences, purchase history, and interests.

This allows you to tailor your upsell and cross-sell offers to specific segments.

3. Craft Relevant Recommendations:

Recommend products or services that are closely related to what the customer has already purchased.

The recommendations should enhance the customer's experience or address their needs.

4. Upselling Strategies:

Upselling involves offering customers a higher-tier product or an upgraded version.

Highlight the added value, features, or benefits of the upgraded option.

5. Cross-Selling Strategies:

Cross-selling involves suggesting complementary products that enhance the customer's main purchase.

Present cross-sell offers as solutions that enhance the primary purchase.

6. Personalized Recommendations:

Use data-driven insights to make personalized recommendations.

Mention how the recommended product complements the customer's previous purchase.

7. Utilize Dynamic Content:

Implement dynamic content in your emails to show personalized product recommendations.

This creates a more engaging and relevant experience for the recipient.

8. Create Bundles and Packages:

Bundle related products together at a discounted rate.

Offer packages that provide a comprehensive solution to the customer's needs.

9. Showcase Benefits:

Clearly communicate the benefits and value of the upsell or cross-sell.

Focus on how the additional product enhances the customer's experience.

10. Highlight Savings:

Emphasize any cost savings or discounts associated with the upsell or cross-sell.

Showcasing value encourages customers to take advantage of the offer.

11. Use Persuasive Language:

Craft persuasive copy that highlights the unique selling points of the additional product.

Use language that encourages the customer to explore the offer further.

12. Incorporate Social Proof:

Include customer testimonials or reviews that validate the effectiveness of the upsell or cross-sell.

Social proof builds trust and confidence in the additional product.

13. Optimize Email Design:

Design visually appealing emails that showcase the products effectively.

Use high-quality images and clear calls-to-action (CTAs).

14. Create Urgency:

Introduce a sense of urgency to encourage prompt action.

Use phrases like "limited-time offer" or "act now" to motivate customers.

15. Test and Analyze:

Test different offers, subject lines, and email layouts.

Analyze the performance of your upsell and cross-sell emails to optimize future campaigns.

By effectively implementing upselling and cross-selling strategies through email marketing, you can enhance customer value, increase revenue per customer, and strengthen customer relationships. Remember that the key is to provide genuine value and focus on addressing the needs and preferences of your customers, ensuring a positive experience that encourages future purchases.

Customer Onboarding and Nurture Campaigns: Cultivating Engagement and Loyalty

Customer onboarding and nurture campaigns are essential components of a successful customer relationship strategy. Onboarding ensures that new customers have a smooth and positive experience with your brand, while nurture campaigns keep existing customers engaged, informed, and loyal over the long term. Through effective email marketing, you can guide customers through their journey and establish lasting connections that lead to repeat purchases and advocacy. Here's how to create customer onboarding and nurture campaigns that multiply sales and foster loyalty:

1. Understand Customer Journeys:

Map out the different stages of your customer journey, from initial awareness to post-purchase.

Tailor your onboarding and nurture campaigns to address the needs and questions at each stage.

2. Personalized Welcome Series:

Design a personalized welcome series for new customers.

Introduce your brand, products, and the value you provide.

3. Provide Guidance:

Guide new customers through their first steps with your product or service.

Offer tutorials, how-to guides, and resources that facilitate a seamless experience.

4. Showcase Value:

Highlight the unique value and benefits of your product or service.

Demonstrate how it solves customers' problems or fulfills their needs.

5. Send Relevant Content:

Segment your customer list and send content that aligns with each segment's interests.

Provide tips, best practices, and industry insights.

6. Exclusive Offers:

Offer exclusive discounts, promotions, or content to nurture engagement.

Make your existing customers feel valued and appreciated.

7. Collect Feedback:

Regularly seek feedback from customers to improve their experience.

Use surveys or feedback emails to gather insights and enhance your offerings.

8. Educational Content:

Share educational content that helps customers get the most out of your product or service.

This can include webinars, video tutorials, and how-to articles.

9. Celebrate Milestones:

Recognize important milestones in your customer relationship, such as anniversaries or achievements.

Send personalized emails to celebrate and thank customers for their loyalty.

10. Ask for Referrals:

Encourage satisfied customers to refer friends and family.

Provide incentives for successful referrals to grow your customer base.

11. Stay Top of Mind:

Regularly send relevant and valuable content to your customers.

Be the go-to resource in your industry, keeping customers engaged with your brand.

12. Use Automation:

Automate the sending of onboarding and nurture emails based on triggers or schedules.

Automation ensures consistent communication without manual effort.

13. Personalized Recommendations:

Provide personalized product recommendations based on customers' preferences and purchase history.

Suggest related products that align with their interests.

14. Loyalty Programs:

Implement a loyalty program that rewards customers for repeat purchases.

Send emails that update customers on their loyalty program status and rewards.

15. Monitor Engagement:

Track engagement metrics like open rates, click-through rates, and responses.

Analyze the data to refine your campaigns and improve customer interactions.

By implementing customer onboarding and nurture campaigns, you can create a strong foundation for customer loyalty and advocacy. These campaigns not only lead to increased sales and revenue but also build lasting relationships that contribute to the overall success of your business. Prioritize understanding your customers' needs, delivering value, and maintaining ongoing communication to create meaningful and impactful campaigns

Abandoned Cart Recovery: Regaining Lost Sales through Email Marketing

Abandoned carts are a common challenge for e-commerce businesses, but they also present a valuable opportunity. Abandoned cart recovery campaigns leverage email marketing to remind customers of items they left behind in their online shopping carts, encouraging them to complete their purchase. These campaigns have the potential to recover lost sales and boost your e-commerce revenue. Here's how to effectively implement abandoned cart recovery strategies through email marketing:

1. Understand the Reasons:

Analyze why customers abandon their carts. Common reasons include unexpected costs, distractions, or comparison shopping.

Understanding the underlying factors helps you tailor your recovery efforts.

2. Capture Email Addresses:

Collect email addresses early in the shopping process, such as during account creation or when items are added to the cart.

Having a valid email address is crucial for sending recovery emails.

3. Timing Matters:

Send the first recovery email shortly after the cart is abandoned.

Follow up with additional emails over a few days, gradually increasing the sense of urgency.

4. Personalize Recovery Emails:

Use the customer's name and reference the items left in the cart.

Personalization increases the chances of re-engagement.

5. Remind of Value:

Highlight the benefits of the abandoned products.

Emphasize features, reviews, or any limited-time offers associated with the items.

6. Offer Incentives:

Include discounts, free shipping, or exclusive offers to entice customers back.

Incentives can tip the balance and motivate customers to complete their purchase.

7. Simplify the Process:

Include a direct link to the abandoned cart.

Make it easy for customers to pick up where they left off.

8. Create a Sense of Urgency:

Use persuasive language that conveys a sense of urgency.

Mention limited stock, impending price changes, or expiration of discounts.

9. Address Concerns:

If customers abandoned due to concerns like shipping costs or return policies, address these issues in your recovery emails.

Provide clear information and solutions to overcome objections.

10. Include Visuals:

Showcase images of the abandoned products.

Visuals remind customers of their selections and reignite their interest.

11. Test Subject Lines and Content:

Experiment with different subject lines, content, and CTAs.

A/B testing helps you identify what resonates best with your audience.

12. Use Abandoned Cart Tools:

Employ e-commerce platforms or email marketing tools that offer abandoned cart recovery features.

These tools automate the process and make it more efficient.

13. Optimize for Mobile:

Ensure that your recovery emails are mobile-responsive.

Many customers check their emails on mobile devices, so a seamless experience is crucial.

14. Monitor and Analyze Results:

Track metrics like open rates, click-through rates, and conversion rates.

Analyze the performance of your recovery emails and make adjustments as needed.

15. Be Persistent but Respectful:

Send a series of recovery emails, but avoid overwhelming customers.

Balance persistence with respectful communication.

Abandoned cart recovery campaigns have the potential to recover a significant portion of otherwise lost sales. By leveraging email marketing to address customer concerns, provide incentives, and create a sense of urgency, you can re-engage potential buyers and encourage them to complete their purchases.

Continuously refine your strategies based on customer behavior and feedback to optimize your abandoned cart recovery efforts.

Advanced Email Marketing Techniques

As your email marketing efforts mature, there's a wealth of advanced techniques and strategies available to take your campaigns to the next level. These techniques are designed to engage your audience on a deeper level, drive conversions, and enhance the overall effectiveness of your email marketing campaigns. From dynamic content and behavioral triggers to segmentation automation and advanced personalization, this section delves into the world of advanced email marketing techniques that can help you achieve exceptional results. By mastering these strategies, you'll be well-equipped to create highly targeted, relevant, and impactful campaigns that maximize your return on investment. Let's explore the advanced techniques that can elevate your email marketing to new heights.

Behavioral Targeting: Delivering Hyper-Relevant Content through Advanced Segmentation

Behavioral targeting is an advanced email marketing technique that allows you to create highly personalized and relevant campaigns based on your subscribers' behaviors, actions, and preferences. By analyzing how subscribers interact with your emails, website, and previous campaigns, you can tailor your content to their specific interests and behaviors. This level of personalization not only boosts engagement but also drives higher conversion rates. Here's how to leverage behavioral targeting to enhance your email marketing efforts:

1. Data Collection:

Gather data on how subscribers interact with your emails and website.

Track metrics like email opens, clicks, website visits, and past purchase history.

2. Segment Based on Behavior:

Segment your email list into groups based on specific behaviors.

For instance, create segments for frequent purchasers, engaged readers, or inactive subscribers.

3. Triggered Campaigns:

Set up triggered email campaigns that respond to specific behaviors.

Examples include abandoned cart emails, post-purchase follow-ups, and re-engagement campaigns.

4. Dynamic Content:

Use dynamic content to customize email content based on subscriber behavior.

Show relevant product recommendations or tailored messaging.

5. Purchase History:

Tailor your emails based on subscribers' past purchase history.

Recommend related products or offer complementary items.

6. Browse Abandonment:

Send emails to subscribers who browse your website without making a purchase.

Recommend products based on their browsing history to re-engage them.

7. Cart Abandonment:

Trigger emails when subscribers add items to their cart but don't complete the purchase.

Remind them of the items in their cart and encourage them to finalize the transaction.

8. Engagement Levels:

Segment subscribers based on their engagement levels with your emails.

Send different content or offers to highly engaged subscribers versus those who are less active.

9. Preferences and Interests:

Analyze subscriber preferences and interests based on their clicks and interactions.

Deliver content that aligns with their preferences, enhancing relevance.

10. Personalized Recommendations:

Provide personalized product recommendations based on past behavior.

Show subscribers items they're likely to be interested in based on their history.

11. Geolocation Targeting:

Use geolocation data to send location-specific offers or promotions.

Tailor content based on subscribers' locations or local events.

12. A/B Testing:

Test different behavioral targeting strategies to optimize results.

Experiment with subject lines, content, and CTAs to determine what resonates best.

13. Nurture Sequences:

Create automated nurture sequences that adapt based on subscriber interactions.

Adjust the content and messaging based on how subscribers engage with your emails.

14. Optimize Over Time:

Continuously monitor and analyze the results of your behavioral targeting campaigns.

Use insights to refine your strategies and improve future campaigns.

15. Maintain Privacy:

Ensure compliance with privacy regulations and obtain explicit consent for tracking behaviors.

Transparently communicate how you use subscriber data to provide a personalized experience.

Behavioral targeting empowers you to deliver content that resonates with subscribers on an individual level. By tailoring your emails to their behaviors and preferences, you can foster stronger relationships, increase engagement, and drive conversions. As you implement behavioral targeting, remember to strike a balance between personalization and privacy, and use data responsibly to create meaningful interactions with your audience.

Dynamic Content Personalization: Elevating Engagement with Tailored Messaging

Dynamic content personalization takes email marketing to a whole new level by allowing you to create emails that adapt and change based on individual subscriber characteristics, behaviors, and preferences. This advanced technique enables you to deliver hyper-relevant content to each recipient, increasing engagement, click-through rates, and conversions. By customizing images, text, and offers in real-time, you can create a unique experience for each subscriber. Here's how to harness the power of dynamic content personalization in your email campaigns:

1. Use Data to Inform Personalization:

Leverage subscriber data such as location, past purchases, and browsing behavior.

Use this data to customize your email content for each recipient.

2. Segment Your Audience:

Divide your email list into segments based on specific attributes or behaviors.

Examples include location, purchase history, engagement levels, and preferences.

3. Customize Images and Offers:

Use dynamic content blocks to display images and offers based on individual preferences.

Show products or promotions that align with the subscriber's interests.

4. Tailor Subject Lines and Preheaders:

Personalize subject lines and preheaders based on subscriber data.

Incorporate their name, location, or product preferences to capture attention.

5. Behavioral Triggers:

Trigger dynamic content based on subscriber behavior or actions.

Send personalized follow-up emails after specific interactions, like cart abandonment.

6. Geolocation Personalization:

Use geolocation data to provide location-specific content.

Display store locations, events, or offers based on the subscriber's location.

7. Product Recommendations:

Incorporate personalized product recommendations based on browsing and purchase history.

Showcase items that the subscriber is likely to be interested in.

8. Dynamic Countdown Timers:

Add countdown timers to create a sense of urgency for limited-time offers.

The timer adjusts in real-time for each recipient, increasing urgency.

9. A/B Testing with Personalization:

Experiment with different dynamic content personalization elements.

A/B test subject lines, images, offers, and other variables to find what works best.

10. Email Interactivity:

Make use of interactive elements like buttons and quizzes.

Create engaging experiences that encourage subscribers to interact with your content.

11. Mobile Responsiveness:

Ensure that your dynamic content is responsive on all devices.

Test your emails on mobile, tablet, and desktop to ensure a seamless experience.

12. Personalized CTA Buttons:

Use dynamic buttons with personalized calls-to-action (CTAs).

Tailor CTAs to each recipient's preferences or stage in the customer journey.

13. Use Merge Tags:

Utilize merge tags to insert subscriber-specific information.

Include their name, location, or other personalized details to create a personal touch.

14. Test and Optimize:

Continuously monitor the performance of your dynamic content campaigns.

Use data-driven insights to optimize your personalization strategy.

15. Respect Privacy:

Always obtain consent and transparently communicate how you use subscriber data.

Prioritize data security and comply with privacy regulations.

Dynamic content personalization transforms your email campaigns into individualized experiences. By delivering content that directly addresses subscribers' interests and needs, you can enhance engagement, build stronger relationships, and ultimately drive higher conversions. Embrace the power of dynamic content personalization to stand out in the inbox and provide a unique journey for each recipient

Advanced Automation Workflows: Orchestrating Multi-Step Campaigns for Optimal Engagement

Advanced automation workflows take email marketing to a sophisticated level by enabling you to design intricate, multi-step campaigns that respond dynamically to subscriber behavior and interactions. These workflows allow you to nurture leads, re-engage customers, and guide subscribers through complex journeys, all while providing a highly personalized experience. By automating each touchpoint along the customer journey, you can ensure consistent and relevant communication that maximizes engagement and conversions. Here's how to leverage advanced automation workflows to enhance your email marketing strategy:

1. Visualize the Customer Journey:

Map out the entire customer journey, identifying touchpoints and interactions.

Visualizing the journey helps you design a seamless automation workflow.

2. Choose an Automation Platform:

Opt for an advanced email marketing platform that offers robust automation capabilities.

Look for features like conditional logic, tagging, and integration options.

3. Define Triggers:

Set up triggers that initiate automation based on specific subscriber actions.

Triggers can include email opens, link clicks, form submissions, and more.

4. Segmentation and Personalization:

Segment your email list based on subscriber behaviors, preferences, and demographics.

Use dynamic content and personalization to tailor your messages.

5. Welcome Series Enhancement:

Build upon basic welcome emails by creating a multi-step welcome series.

Gradually introduce your brand, products, and value over several emails.

6. Lead Nurturing Campaigns:

Design workflows that nurture leads through their decision-making process.

Deliver relevant content at each stage to educate and guide prospects.

7. Abandoned Cart Recovery Sequence:

Set up a sequence for abandoned cart recovery.

Send a series of emails to remind customers of their abandoned carts and encourage conversion.

8. Re-Engagement Workflows:

Automate workflows to re-engage inactive subscribers.

Send targeted emails to reignite interest and prompt reactivation.

9. Drip Campaigns:

Create drip campaigns that deliver a series of emails over a set schedule.

Guide subscribers through a predetermined sequence of content and offers.

10. Behavioral Triggers:

Set up triggers that respond to specific subscriber actions.

For example, send a follow-up email after a certain link click or website visit.

11. Conditional Logic:

Use conditional logic to tailor the workflow based on subscriber responses.

Adapt the content and next steps based on their choices.

12. Lead Scoring and Tagging:

Implement lead scoring to assign values to different subscriber behaviors.

Tag subscribers based on their interactions to tailor future communications.

13. Product Recommendations:

Incorporate dynamic product recommendations based on browsing and purchase history.

Showcase items aligned with the subscriber's interests.

14. A/B Testing in Workflows:

Experiment with different subject lines, content, and CTAs within your automation workflows.

A/B testing helps you optimize the performance of each step.

15. Monitor and Adjust:

Continuously monitor the performance of your automation workflows.

Analyze engagement metrics and make adjustments to optimize results.

Advanced automation workflows allow you to engage with your audience in a highly targeted and personalized manner. By responding to their behaviors and delivering content that aligns with their interests, you can build stronger relationships, increase conversions, and enhance customer satisfaction.

As you create and refine your advanced automation workflows, ensure that your communication remains relevant, timely, and valuable to your subscribers at every stage of their journey

Integration with Other Marketing Channels: Unifying Strategies for Comprehensive Impact

Integration with other marketing channels is a powerful approach that involves aligning your email marketing efforts with other digital marketing channels, such as social media, content marketing, and advertising. This strategy ensures consistency across your campaigns, maximizes your reach, and enhances the overall effectiveness of your marketing initiatives. By creating a cohesive and unified customer experience, you can multiply your results and achieve a comprehensive impact. Here's how to seamlessly integrate email marketing with other channels for optimal outcomes:

1. Cross-Channel Strategy:

Develop a comprehensive marketing strategy that incorporates email marketing and other channels.

Define how each channel will work together to achieve your overall goals.

2. Consistent Branding:

Maintain consistent branding and messaging across all channels.

Ensure that your brand identity remains cohesive to provide a seamless customer experience.

3. Content Integration:

Align your email content with your content marketing strategy.

Share blog posts, articles, and other valuable content through both email and other channels.

4. Social Media Integration:

Include social media buttons and links in your emails.

Share your email content on social media platforms to extend its reach.

5. Retargeting and Advertising:

Use email data to retarget subscribers with relevant ads.

Create custom audiences for your advertising campaigns based on your email list.

6. Landing Page Consistency:

Ensure that the landing pages linked from your emails align with the email content.

Maintain a consistent message and design to avoid confusion.

7. Multi-Channel Campaigns:

Plan campaigns that run across multiple channels simultaneously.

Coordinate messaging and offers to create a unified experience for your audience.

8. Event Promotion:

Use email to promote events, and share event content on social media.

Cross-promotion helps maximize attendance and engagement.

9. Data Sharing and Integration:

Integrate data from various channels to create a unified customer profile.

This data-driven approach enables better targeting and personalization.

10. Email Opt-Ins from Other Channels:

Collect email opt-ins from social media, website forms, and other channels.

Grow your email list by leveraging your presence on other platforms.

11. Coordinated Campaigns:

Coordinate the timing and messaging of your email campaigns with other channels.

Deliver consistent messages across channels to reinforce your campaign's impact.

12. Unified Reporting:

Analyze performance data from all integrated channels.

Gain insights into how each channel contributes to overall engagement and conversions.

13. Retention and Loyalty:

Use email marketing to reinforce customer loyalty strategies from other channels.

Reward loyal customers and provide exclusive offers through email.

14. Test and Optimize:

Experiment with different integration approaches to find what works best for your audience.

Continuously optimize your integrated strategies based on performance data.

15. Customer Feedback Loop:

Use feedback from various channels to improve your email campaigns.

Insights from social media, customer support, and other sources can inform your messaging.

Integration with other marketing channels creates a holistic and impactful approach to engaging with your audience. By delivering a consistent message and experience across different touchpoints, you can amplify your reach and influence, ultimately multiplying your results. Embrace the synergy between email marketing and other channels to create a seamless journey for your customers and enhance the effectiveness of your overall marketing strategy.

Staying Updated with Email Marketing Trends

In the dynamic landscape of digital marketing, staying informed about the latest trends and developments is essential to keep your email marketing strategies relevant and effective. The field of email marketing is constantly evolving, driven by changes in consumer behavior, technological advancements, and shifting industry norms. By staying updated with the latest trends, you can adapt your strategies to meet the evolving needs of your audience and maintain a competitive edge. In this section, we'll explore the importance of staying current with email marketing trends and how doing so can empower you to continually optimize your campaigns and achieve exceptional results. Let's delve into the world of email marketing trends and their impact on your strategies.

Responsive Design and Mobile Optimization: Adapting to the Mobile-First Era

In today's digital landscape, where mobile devices are ubiquitous, responsive design and mobile optimization have become crucial elements of successful email marketing. With a significant portion of email opens occurring on mobile devices, it's imperative to ensure that your email campaigns are designed and optimized for a seamless mobile experience. Failing to do so can lead to decreased engagement and missed opportunities. Let's explore the importance of responsive design and mobile optimization in email marketing and how you can leverage these practices to reach and engage your audience effectively:

1. Mobile-First Approach:

Design your emails with a mobile-first mindset.

Prioritize mobile optimization to cater to the growing number of mobile users.

2. Responsive Design:

Use responsive design techniques to create emails that adapt to different screen sizes.

Ensure your emails look great and are easily readable on both small and large screens.

3. Simple Layouts:

Opt for clean and simple email layouts.

Avoid clutter and focus on delivering a concise message that resonates with mobile users.

4. Short and Engaging Content:

Craft concise and engaging content that captures attention quickly.

Mobile users have limited attention spans, so every word counts.

5. Clear Calls-to-Action (CTAs):

Make your CTAs prominent and easy to tap.

Use large buttons with contrasting colors to encourage interaction.

6. Optimized Images:

Use images that load quickly and look sharp on mobile screens.

Compress images to reduce loading times without compromising quality.

7. Minimalistic Formatting:

Avoid excessive use of fonts, colors, and formatting.

A simple and consistent design enhances readability on mobile devices.

8. Preview and Testing:

Use preview and testing tools to see how your emails appear on different devices.

Ensure that images, text, and buttons are appropriately sized and aligned.

9. Touch-Friendly Elements:

Design buttons and links with enough spacing to prevent accidental taps.

Consider the ease of interaction for users navigating with their fingers.

10. Single Column Layouts:

Opt for single-column layouts to provide a linear reading experience.

Single-column designs work well on mobile screens, minimizing the need for scrolling.

11. Prioritize Load Times:

Keep file sizes small to ensure fast loading times.

Slow-loading emails can lead to user frustration and abandonment.

12. Preheader Optimization:

Craft compelling preheaders that complement the subject line.

Preheaders provide additional context and encourage mobile users to open your emails.

13. Testing on Multiple Devices:

Test your emails on various mobile devices and email clients.

Ensure consistent rendering and functionality across different platforms.

14. Continuous Optimization:

Regularly review and optimize your mobile email templates.

Stay updated with new design techniques and best practices.

15. Monitor Analytics:

Monitor mobile engagement metrics such as open rates, click-through rates, and conversions.

Use data insights to refine your mobile optimization strategies.

Responsive design and mobile optimization are no longer optional; they are essential for delivering a positive user experience and achieving optimal email engagement. By catering to the needs of mobile users, you can ensure that your email campaigns are effective across all devices, leading to higher open rates, better engagement, and ultimately, improved conversions. As mobile usage continues to grow, embracing these practices will be a key driver of your email marketing success

Interactive Email Elements: Engaging and Immersive Email Experiences

Interactive email elements represent a cutting-edge approach to email marketing, allowing you to transform static emails into interactive and engaging experiences. By incorporating interactive elements such as buttons, carousels, quizzes, and more, you can captivate your audience's attention and encourage them to interact directly within the email itself. This advanced technique not only boosts engagement but also provides a unique and memorable experience that sets your emails apart from the competition. Let's explore the world of interactive email elements and how you can leverage them to create immersive and engaging email campaigns:

1. Engage with Interactivity:

Capture subscribers' attention with interactive elements that invite them to interact within the email.

Encourage users to take actions directly from the email itself.

2. Interactive Buttons:

Replace static buttons with interactive ones.

Incorporate hover effects, changing colors, or animations to make buttons more engaging.

3. Image Carousels:

Use image carousels to showcase multiple products or features in a single email.

Allow recipients to swipe through the carousel to explore different options.

4. Accordion Menus:

Utilize accordion menus to provide additional content within the email.

Let subscribers expand and collapse sections to access more information.

5. Surveys and Polls:

Embed surveys or polls directly into your emails.

Gather feedback, preferences, or opinions from your subscribers.

6. Quizzes and Games:

Create interactive quizzes or simple games within your emails.

Gamification adds an element of fun and engagement to your campaigns.

7. Countdown Timers:

Incorporate countdown timers to create a sense of urgency.

Encourage subscribers to take immediate action before the timer runs out.

8. Product Hover Effects:

Add product images that expand or show additional information when hovered over.

Provide a sneak peek without requiring the recipient to click through.

9. Interactive Forms:

Embed forms for event registrations, surveys, or feedback directly within the email.

Allow users to submit information without leaving the email.

10. Video Previews:

Include video previews or GIFs to showcase video content.

Give recipients a taste of your video content without needing to click away.

11. Interactive Hotspots:

Design emails with interactive hotspots that reveal additional information when clicked.

Create an interactive map or image that engages subscribers.

12. Personalized Recommendations:

Use interactive elements to provide personalized product recommendations.

Let subscribers explore different options within the email.

13. Progress Bars:

Include progress bars for courses, challenges, or account setup.

Show subscribers their progress and encourage them to complete tasks.

14. Live Social Media Feeds:

Integrate live social media feeds directly into your emails.

Showcase your latest posts and encourage subscribers to follow you.

15. Testing and Optimization:

Experiment with different interactive elements to see what resonates with your audience.

Continuously optimize your interactive emails based on engagement metrics.

Interactive email elements not only captivate subscribers' attention but also drive higher engagement and interaction rates. By creating emails that encourage recipients to engage directly within the email itself, you can provide a more immersive experience and stand out in crowded inboxes. As email clients continue to support more interactive features, embracing this trend can lead to improved results and enhanced customer experiences

Video in Emails: Enhancing Engagement with Multimedia Content

Video has become a dominant form of online content consumption, and incorporating video into your email campaigns can significantly enhance engagement and captivate your audience. Video in emails adds a dynamic and interactive dimension that traditional text and images alone cannot achieve. By leveraging video content, you can deliver your message in a more engaging and memorable way, ultimately driving higher click-through rates, conversions, and overall campaign success. Let's explore the benefits of using video in emails and how you can effectively integrate this multimedia content into your email marketing strategy:

1. Captivating Visual Content:

Videos capture attention and convey information more effectively than text.

Engage recipients with visually appealing and dynamic content.

2. Improved Engagement:

Video content leads to higher engagement rates compared to static content.

Encourage recipients to spend more time interacting with your email.

3. Enhanced Storytelling:

Tell a compelling brand or product story through video.

Use visuals, music, and narration to create a captivating narrative.

4. Product Demonstrations:

Showcase product features and benefits through video demonstrations.

Provide a clear and detailed view of how your product works.

5. Event Recaps and Highlights:

Share event recaps, highlights, or behind-the-scenes footage through videos.

Provide subscribers with an immersive experience of your events.

6. Video Previews:

Include video previews that tease upcoming content or promotions.

Encourage subscribers to click through to watch the full video.

7. Video Testimonials:

Use video testimonials from satisfied customers to build trust.

Visual testimonials have a more significant impact than written ones.

8. Video Landing Pages:

Embed video content within your email that links to a dedicated landing page.

Drive traffic to your website where users can engage further.

9. Animated GIFs:

Use animated GIFs to provide a snippet of video content.

GIFs work well in emails and can act as teaser trailers for your full video.

10. Personalized Videos:

Create personalized videos for individual subscribers.

Include the recipient's name or specific information to increase engagement.

11. Hosting Platforms:

Host your videos on reliable platforms such as YouTube or Vimeo.

Embed video links or thumbnails in your emails to maintain a professional appearance.

12. Clear Call-to-Action:

Include a clear and compelling call-to-action (CTA) that prompts users to watch the video.

Use attention-grabbing CTAs to encourage clicks.

13. Mobile Compatibility:

Ensure that your video content is mobile-responsive.

Many recipients view emails on mobile devices, so seamless mobile playback is crucial.

14. Thumbnail Selection:

Choose an engaging and relevant video thumbnail.

Thumbnails can significantly influence whether recipients choose to watch the video.

15. Test and Analyze:

Experiment with different types of video content and placements.

Analyze engagement metrics to determine the impact of video on your campaigns.

Integrating video into your email campaigns allows you to create a richer and more immersive experience for your subscribers. By utilizing the power of visual storytelling and engaging multimedia content, you can increase audience engagement, drive conversions, and strengthen your brand's connection with your audience. As the popularity of video content continues to grow, leveraging video in your emails can provide a competitive advantage and set your campaigns apart

AI and Machine Learning in Email Marketing: Elevating Personalization and Automation

The integration of artificial intelligence (AI) and machine learning (ML) into email marketing has revolutionized how brands engage with their audiences. These technologies enable marketers to deliver highly personalized and relevant content, automate complex tasks, and make data-driven decisions that drive better results. By harnessing the power of AI and ML, you can enhance the efficiency and effectiveness of your email marketing campaigns. Let's explore how AI and machine learning are shaping the future of email marketing and how you can leverage these technologies to optimize your strategies:

1. Personalization at Scale:

AI analyzes vast amounts of data to create hyper-personalized content.

Tailor emails based on subscriber behavior, preferences, and demographics.

2. Predictive Analytics:

Use ML algorithms to predict subscriber behavior and preferences.

Anticipate what content and offers will resonate most with individual recipients.

3. Subject Line Optimization:

AI can analyze past open rates and optimize subject lines.

Create compelling subject lines that boost open rates and engagement.

4. Content Recommendations:

ML algorithms analyze user behavior to suggest relevant content.

Provide subscribers with content recommendations based on their interests

5. Send Time Optimization:

Use AI to determine the best time to send emails to each subscriber.

Increase the likelihood of your emails being seen and engaged with.

6. Dynamic Content Generation:

AI can generate personalized content dynamically.

Create individualized product recommendations, offers, and more.

7. List Segmentation:

Machine learning helps segment your audience more accurately.

Identify distinct segments based on behavior, demographics, and engagement.

8. Churn Prediction:

Predict which subscribers are at risk of churning.

Take proactive measures to re-engage and retain these subscribers.

9. A/B Testing Automation:

AI can automate A/B testing and identify winning variations.

Optimize your campaigns without manual intervention.

10. Behavioral Triggers:

Use AI to trigger emails based on specific subscriber actions.

Send timely and relevant follow-up emails based on behaviors.

11. Customer Journey Mapping:

AI helps map out customer journeys and touchpoints.

Design campaigns that align with each stage of the customer journey.

12. Data Analysis and Insights:

AI can process and analyze large datasets quickly.

Gain valuable insights into subscriber behavior and campaign performance.

13. Fraud Detection:

Use AI to detect and prevent email fraud and phishing attacks.

Enhance the security of your email communications.

14. Automation of Repetitive Tasks:

AI-powered automation handles routine tasks like list cleaning and data entry.

Free up your time to focus on strategic planning and creative tasks.

15. Continuous Learning and Improvement:

AI and ML systems learn and adapt over time.

Improve the accuracy and effectiveness of your campaigns through continuous learning.

AI and machine learning have the potential to transform your email marketing from a static broadcast to a dynamic and personalized experience. By harnessing the insights and capabilities of these technologies, you can deliver content that resonates with individual subscribers, optimize your strategies based on data-driven insights, and achieve higher levels of engagement and conversion. As AI and machine learning continue to evolve, integrating them into your email marketing strategy can keep you at the forefront of industry innovation

Case Studies of Successful Email Marketing Campaigns

Learning from real-world examples is a valuable way to gain insights into what works in email marketing. Examining successful email marketing campaigns provides a practical understanding of effective strategies, creative approaches, and the impact of thoughtful execution. In this section, we will delve into a selection of case studies that showcase various aspects of email marketing success. These case studies highlight how different businesses leveraged email marketing to achieve their goals, engage their audience, and drive impressive results. By exploring these success stories, you can draw inspiration and apply proven techniques to your own email marketing endeavors. Let's dive into the world of successful email marketing campaigns and uncover the strategies that propelled these businesses to achievement.

Real-World Examples and Lessons Learned: Uncovering Strategies for Success

In the realm of email marketing, learning from the experiences of others can be incredibly insightful. Real-world examples provide tangible evidence of effective strategies and the impact of well-executed campaigns. Let's explore a selection of real-world examples and the valuable lessons they offer for your own email marketing efforts:

1. Airbnb: Creating Personalized Recommendations

Campaign: Airbnb sends personalized recommendations to users based on their search history and preferences.

Lesson: Leveraging user data to provide tailored content increases engagement and encourages repeat interactions.

2. BuzzFeed: Crafting Curiosity-Driven Subject Lines

Campaign: BuzzFeed employs curiosity-driven subject lines to entice recipients to open their emails.

Lesson: Creative and intriguing subject lines can significantly boost open rates and pique subscriber interest.

3. Dropbox: Referral Program Success

Campaign: Dropbox's "refer-a-friend" campaign rewards users for referring new customers.

Lesson: Incentive-based referral programs can foster word-of-mouth marketing and user growth.

4. Nike: Combining Personalization and Urgency

Campaign: Nike sends personalized emails featuring products left in the shopping cart, along with a countdown timer.

Lesson: Combining personalization and urgency can motivate customers to complete purchases.

5. Grammarly: Educational Content and User Engagement

Campaign: Grammarly sends grammar tips and educational content to its subscribers.

Lesson: Providing value-added educational content can foster a loyal audience and build trust.

6. TheSkimm: Nurturing Engagement through Storytelling

Campaign: TheSkimm's newsletter combines news updates with engaging storytelling.

Lesson: Engaging storytelling can transform routine content into captivating experiences.

7. Starbucks: Seasonal Promotions and Exclusivity

Campaign: Starbucks offers exclusive promotions and seasonal offerings to its loyalty program members.

Lesson: Creating a sense of exclusivity and capitalizing on seasons can drive engagement and sales.

8. Warby Parker: Customer Testimonials and Social Proof

Campaign: Warby Parker features customer testimonials and social proof in its emails.

Lesson: Incorporating real customer stories and positive feedback can build trust and credibility.

9. Casper: Interactive Content for Engagement

Campaign: Casper uses interactive quizzes to engage subscribers and understand their preferences.

Lesson: Interactive content can foster engagement and provide insights into customer preferences.

10. Charity: Water: Impactful Storytelling for Donations

- Campaign: Charity: Water uses emotional storytelling to inspire donations and support.

- Lesson: Powerful storytelling can create an emotional connection and motivate action.

11. Amazon: Behavior-Based Recommendations

- Campaign: Amazon suggests products based on users' browsing and purchase history.

- Lesson: Utilizing behavior-based recommendations can drive personalized engagement and sales.

12. Spotify: Curated Personalized Playlists

- Campaign: Spotify shares personalized music playlists with users based on their listening history.

- Lesson: Curating content based on user preferences can enhance engagement and satisfaction.

13. Domino's: Interactive and Engaging Content

- Campaign: Domino's uses interactive features to let users customize their pizza orders.

- Lesson: Interactive elements enhance engagement and user experience, leading to higher conversions.

By dissecting these real-world examples, you can glean actionable insights that apply to your own email marketing campaigns. Each case study highlights a unique strategy, approach, or tactic that contributed to campaign success. Consider how you can adapt these lessons to your brand, audience, and goals, and incorporate the elements that resonate most effectively with your subscribers

Conclusion: Mastering the Art of Email Marketing

Email marketing is a dynamic and ever-evolving field that holds immense potential for businesses to connect with their audience, drive engagement, and achieve remarkable results. In this comprehensive guide, we've explored the intricacies of email marketing, from crafting compelling content to leveraging advanced strategies and technologies. Here's a recap of the key takeaways from each section:

Introduction to Email Marketing: Email marketing remains a powerful tool for businesses to engage with their audience and drive conversions. Its versatility and effectiveness make it a cornerstone of digital marketing strategies.

Building Your Email Marketing Strategy: A well-defined strategy is the foundation of successful email marketing. Understand your target audience, set clear goals, choose the right platform, and create a plan that aligns with your business objectives.

Creating an Effective Email List: Building a high-quality email list requires careful attention to permission-based marketing, segmentation, and personalized content that resonates with subscribers.

Crafting Compelling Email Content: Crafting engaging content involves attention to subject lines, email design, relevant and valuable information, persuasive CTAs, and visual appeal.

Automation and Segmentation: Automation enhances efficiency, while segmentation and personalization ensure that your messages are tailored to the specific needs and behaviors of your subscribers.

Avoiding Common Email Marketing Mistakes: Steer clear of common pitfalls like spam filters, frequency overkill, and insufficient A/B testing to maintain positive subscriber engagement.

Compliance and Legal Considerations: Understand and adhere to regulations such as the CAN-SPAM Act and GDPR to ensure privacy, data protection, and ethical practices.

Measuring and Analyzing Email Campaigns: Track key metrics, analyze data, and use analytics to optimize your campaigns for improved engagement and ROI.

Beginner's Guide to Starting Email Marketing: Start by building your email list, crafting initial content, and setting up basic automated campaigns to kickstart your email marketing journey.

Strategies to Multiply Sales and Leads: Utilize irresistible offers, upselling and cross-selling tactics, customer onboarding, and abandoned cart recovery to drive conversions and increase leads.

Advanced Email Marketing Techniques: Leverage behavioral targeting, dynamic content personalization, and advanced automation workflows for sophisticated and highly effective campaigns.

Staying Updated with Email Marketing Trends: Stay current with trends like responsive design, interactive elements, video content, AI, and machine learning to keep your campaigns relevant and effective.

Case Studies of Successful Email Marketing Campaigns: Learn from real-world examples and apply the lessons learned to optimize your email marketing strategies.

As you embark on your email marketing journey, remember that success requires continuous learning, adaptation, and a commitment to delivering value to your subscribers. By employing the strategies and techniques outlined in this guide and staying attuned to the ever-changing landscape of email marketing, you can forge stronger connections with your audience, increase engagement, and achieve your business goals. Email marketing is not just a means of communication; it's an art that, when mastered, can transform your business's online presence and drive remarkable growth.

Encouragement for Beginners to Start: Embrace the Power of Email Marketing

To those who are new to the world of email marketing, embarking on this journey might feel like stepping into uncharted territory. However, with the right guidance and a willingness to learn, you have the potential to unlock a world of opportunities and connect with your audience in ways you never thought possible. Here's a dose of encouragement to inspire you as you take your first steps into the realm of email marketing:

1. You're Joining a Proven Tradition:

Email marketing has stood the test of time as one of the most reliable and effective forms of communication. It's a tradition that has evolved with technology, making it a versatile tool for businesses of all sizes.

2. Start Small, Dream Big:

You don't need to send massive campaigns right from the beginning. Start with a small, engaged list and gradually scale your efforts as you learn and grow.

3. Learning Curve is Your Friend:

Every expert was once a beginner. Embrace the learning curve and allow yourself to make mistakes. It's through these experiences that you'll gain valuable insights and become more skilled over time.

4. Personalization is Your Superpower:

Your uniqueness and understanding of your audience are your greatest assets. Tailor your content to resonate with your subscribers, and watch as your engagement rates soar.

5. Automation Empowers You:

Automation takes the load off your shoulders and lets you focus on creativity and strategy. As a beginner, automation can make your campaigns efficient and effective.

6. Success Stories Await:

Many successful businesses started right where you are now. Allow their stories to inspire you, knowing that your dedication and effort can lead to your own success story.

7. Test, Test, and Test Again:

Testing is your secret weapon. Experiment with different subject lines, content, and strategies. Your ability to adapt and optimize will set you on the path to success.

8. Your Audience Wants to Hear from You:

Your subscribers have opted in because they want to hear from you. They're interested in your content and what you have to offer. Deliver value, and they'll reward you with their attention.

9. Incremental Progress Matters:

Celebrate every small victory along the way. Whether it's an increase in open rates, engagement, or conversions, each step forward is a step closer to achieving your goals.

10. You're Not Alone:

There's a wealth of resources, guides, and communities out there to support you. Join forums, connect with fellow marketers, and tap into the collective knowledge of the email marketing community.

11. Adapt and Thrive:

The landscape of email marketing is always evolving. Embrace new trends, technologies, and strategies. Adaptation is the key to staying relevant and achieving long-term success.

12. Consistency is Key:

Consistency breeds familiarity and trust. Stick to a regular email schedule, and you'll build a reliable connection with your subscribers.

13. Learn from Your Audience:

Your subscribers are a valuable source of feedback. Pay attention to their responses, engagement, and preferences. Use this information to refine your approach.

14. Embrace Your Creativity:

Email marketing is an art as much as it is a science. Use your creativity to craft compelling content that stands out in crowded inboxes.

15. Celebrate Progress, Not Perfection:

Perfection isn't the goal; progress is. Every campaign, every interaction, and every lesson learned contributes to your growth as an email marketer.

Remember, every successful email marketer started as a beginner. The key is to take that first step, remain open to learning, and be persistent in your efforts. Your journey in email marketing will be a rewarding one, filled with opportunities to connect, engage, and ultimately, make a positive impact on your audience and your business. So, go ahead, embrace the power of email marketing, and watch as your efforts blossom into something truly remarkable

About the Author

 **Ramindev Murali Anand**

Ramindev Murali Anand is a seasoned digital marketing expert, visionary strategist, and passionate advocate for the power of email marketing. With over a decade of experience in the field, Ramindev has established himself as a trusted authority, guiding businesses of all sizes towards harnessing the potential of email campaigns to foster connections, drive engagement, and achieve remarkable results.

Drawing on a diverse background that encompasses marketing, technology, and consumer behavior, Ramindev has honed a unique perspective that seamlessly blends creativity with data-driven insights. His commitment to staying at the forefront of industry trends, combined with his dedication to empowering others, has led to a reputation as an influential thought leader in the realm of email marketing.

Ramindev's approach to email marketing is rooted in the belief that every email is an opportunity to tell a story, to engage, and to provide value. His ability to craft compelling narratives and translate complex concepts into accessible strategies has resonated with both novices and experts alike. Through speaking engagements, workshops, and consulting, Ramindev has inspired countless individuals to embrace email marketing as an art form—a medium through which businesses can authentically connect with their audience.

As the author of this comprehensive guide, Ramindev Murali Anand brings his extensive expertise to the forefront, offering readers a roadmap to navigate the intricacies of email marketing. His commitment to clarity, practicality, and empowering others shines through in every chapter. With each insight shared, practical tip offered, and real-world case study analyzed, Ramindev's goal is to provide readers with the tools and knowledge they need to master the art of email marketing and achieve their marketing objectives.

With Ramindev Murali Anand as your guide, you are embarking on a journey of discovery and growth in the world of email marketing. Through his expertise, dedication, and passion for the subject, you'll be equipped to not only understand the nuances of effective email campaigns but also to craft strategies that leave a lasting impact on your audience and your business.

www.ingramcontent.com/pod-product-compliance
Lightning Source LLC
Chambersburg PA
CBHW080244280726
48661CB00023B/3898